Edward de Bono is the leading authority in the field of creative thinking and the direct teaching of thinking as a skill. While there are thousands of people writing software for computers, Edward de Bono is the pioneer in writing software for the human brain. From an understanding of how the human brain works as a self-organising information system, he derived the formal creative tools of lateral thinking. He is also the originator of 'parallel thinking' and the Six Thinking Hats. His tools for perceptual thinking (CoRT and DAAT) are widely used in both schools and business.

Edward de Bono's instruction in thinking has been sought by many of the leading corporations in the world such as IBM, Microsoft, Prudential, BT (UK), NTT (Japan), Nokia (Finland) and Siemens (Germany). The Australian national cricket team also sought his help and became the most successful cricket team in history.

A group of academics in South Africa included Dr de Bono as one of the 250 people who had most influenced humanity in the whole course of history. A leading Austrian business journal chose him as one of the twenty visionaries alive today. The leading consultancy company, Accenture, chose him as one of the fifty most influential business thinkers today.

Edward de Bono's methods are simple but powerful. The use of just one method produced 21,000 ideas for a steel company in one afternoon. He has taught thinking to Nobel prize winners and Down's syndrome youngsters.

Edward de Bono holds an MD (Malta), MA (Oxford), DPhil (Oxford), PhD (Cambridge) and Ddes (RMIT). He has had faculty appointments at the universities of Oxford, Cambridge, London and Harvard and was a Rhodes Scholar at Oxford. He has written 67 books with translations into 37 languages.

THE
SIX
VALUE
MEDALS

EDWARD DE BONO

LONDON

First published in the United Kingdom in 2005 by
Vermilion, an imprint of Ebury Publishing
Random House UK Ltd
Random House
20 Vauxhall Bridge Road
London SW1V 2SA

Random House Australia (Pty) Limited
20 Alfred Street, Milsons Point, Sydney
New South Wales 2061, Australia

Random House New Zealand Limited
18 Poland Road, Glenfield
Auckland 10, New Zealand

Random House (Pty) Limited
Endulini, 5A Jubilee Road, Parktown 2193, South Africa

Random House UK Limited Reg. No. 954009

www.randomhouse.co.uk

Papers used by Vermilion are natural, recyclable products
made from wood grown in sustainable forests.

A CIP catalogue record is available for this book
from the British Library.

ISBN: 009189459X

Printed and bound in Great Britain by
Mackays of Chatham plc, Chatham, Kent

●●●●●●

CONTENTS

17 The Value Triangle   143

18 The Value Map   153

VICTERI Teams   159

Conclusion   161

INTRODUCTION:

What Are the Six Value Medals?

We can greatly improve our traditional thinking habits. Traditional thinking is all about analysis and judgment. We recognise standard situations and apply standard answers. This is no longer enough. You can analyse the past but you have to design the future.

Values come into all areas of thinking and behaviour. Values are what we consider important, but we may not be consciously aware of them.

This book provides a powerful framework for value assessment. Different types of value are given broad category names: gold, silver, steel, glass, wood and brass. This makes it easier for us to notice such values, to look for them, to see them and to act upon them.

I have generally referred to applying the six value medals to organisations. Businesses, managers and employees will all benefit from them but they work just as well when an individual is the organisation. You can apply these values to all areas of your life.

Why We Need Values

I have worked with many of the world's major corporations: IBM, DuPont, Exxon, Shell, Nokia, Motorola, NTT, British Telecom, GM, Ford, etc. In many cases management seems to work on the basis of maintenance and problem-solving. This means keep going as you are going and solve problems as they arise. To this might be added mergers, acquisitions and 'me-too' behaviour – if another company innovates successfully, you follow with your own version.

Who is to say that this is not a successful strategy? Something that seems satisfactory at the moment may not continue to be so. Corporations that are satisfied with 'maintenance and problem-solving' may be operating far below their potential.

Commodities

Three things are becoming commodities in business:

1 **Competence** is becoming a commodity. Not all
    organisations are equally competent but they are all
    moving that way. If your only hope of survival is that
    you will continue to be more competent than your
    competitors, this is a weak basis for survival. It is
    weak because there is nothing you can do to stop
    your competitors from becoming as competent as
    your organisation. You may keep ahead but the

amount by which you keep ahead will get smaller and smaller.

2 **Information** *is becoming a commodity. You can readily obtain information and buy it if necessary. Secrets are rather rare. You may get some special information ahead of others but they will also get that information in due course. Computers and the internet mean the end of private information.*

3 **State-of-the-art technology** *is also becoming a commodity. Technology can be bought, commissioned and surpassed. It may be that in a few areas, such as pharmaceuticals, special technology will give a lead – but that is rare. In any case, technology by itself is useless unless turned into value. The world does not need gadgets that are more gadgety but ones that deliver real value.*

Similarly, on an individual level, it is no longer enough to be competent, informed and computer literate. These skills are now taken as read by employers. To forge ahead in our careers we need to add value to what we can offer.

So if everything is becoming a commodity available to everyone, what is going to make the difference?

The Cooking Competition

Imagine a cooking competition with six champion chefs at a long table. Each of these chefs has exactly the same ingredients. Each has the same cooking facilities. Who wins the competition?

You may suggest that the winner will be the chef that cooks exactly the same dish as every other chef but cooks it much better.

More likely, the winner will be the chef who takes the same ingredients and turns them into superior value by cooking a dish the others had not considered.

> **When everything becomes a commodity what is going to matter is the ability to design and deliver value. That needs creative and design thinking.**

Changes in Thinking

A major corporation in Finland used to spend thirty days on their multi-national project discussions. Using the parallel thinking method (Six Hats) designed by the author, they now complete the process in two days.

MDS in Canada reckoned they saved $20 million the first year they used parallel thinking.

Siemens, in Germany, estimated that they had reduced their product development time by fifty percent through using this thinking.

A number of workshops set up for a steel company in South Africa generated 21,000 ideas in a single

afternoon using just one of the techniques of lateral thinking.

The employment rate of unemployed youngsters in the UK was increased fivefold after just six hours of instruction in better thinking methods.

Thinking about Value

It is not the purpose of this book to tell people and organisations how to act on their values. The purpose is to make it easier for people to think about their values. New ways of thinking about value are put forward. New frameworks are provided.

In the end, human thinking is the most important resource we have, and there is a great deal of room for improvement. This book puts forward new ways of thinking about value and provides new frameworks. It introduces the six value medals then shows you how to apply them. You will learn to score and map your values, providing an essential tool for decision-making in all aspects of your life.

VALUES

When Do We Need to Assess Values?

Almost any thinking and almost any action has an important value component. It is impossible to ignore values. Every decision we make involves values.

Decisions

There are, broadly, two types of decision:

1 *Decide whether or not to do something. You decide to move forward from where you are or decide to stay put.*
2 *A choice between alternatives (which may also include doing nothing).*

When considering whether to move ahead with a new product, a new service or a new project – or when making decisions in your personal life – there is a need to assess values:

- *Will this project be profitable?*
- *How will the project impact existing operations?*
- *What will customers perceive as value?*
- *How will this affect the competitive position of our organisation?*
- *How will this affect the environment?*

On a personal level you might ask:

- *How will this affect my happiness?*
- *How will this affect my family?*
- *How will this affect my finances?*

There would be many more such questions.

Each question asks for an assessment of a certain type of value. If the values are not there, or if the values are negative (see page 21), then the project may not be worth considering or doing. It is possible that a very high value in one area may override a weak value in other areas. In general, however, the overall value is only as strong as the weakest value (like the links in a chain). Something that is profitable but has low customer values is not likely to be a success. Something that pleases customers but upsets the workforce is not a good idea. Something that has high values everywhere else but damages the environment is best avoided. Something that makes you happy but seriously inconveniences your family may not be worth pursuing.

Value Scanning

With decisions that are really choices between alternatives, each of the alternatives needs to be scanned for value. A comparison of the value scans then forms the basis of the decision. Should a country focus on large-volume, mass-market tourism, or on high-end, high-spend tourism?

If decisions are not based on values there are not many other bases. You can make a decision because you are told to or are pressured to by others or by public opinion. You can make decisions in a routine fashion according to some signal. You can make decisions based not on the facts of the matter but on your sense of style ('that is the sort of decision I always make'). This 'style' form of decision-making has been the downfall of many very successful politicians. You can make decisions on a random basis and then seek to put them right as things go along.

> **If values affect all our thinking then it makes sense to do a value scan and to identify the values we use for decisions.**

Just as a small-scale builder would use a spirit level to check something was level, so we need to make frequent value checks on our decisions to make sure things turn out right.

We will now look at some of the many situations in which value scanning is essential. This will give you a feel for the importance of assessing the values in all your decisions, both business and personal. Later in the book you will meet each of the six value medals in detail and then I will show you how to carry out a value scan.

CHOICE OF IDEAS

Creative thinking and deliberate lateral thinking often turn up a large number of new ideas. How do we assess these ideas? Which ones need further thought? Which ones are promising? Which ones do we take to the next step? Which ones do we invest in?

The answer to all these questions is based on a value scan. What do the values look like in each case?

A new idea may be noticed just because it is new and different. But if there are no other values, 'newness' may not be enough.

ALLOCATION OF RESOURCES

There are usually insufficient resources to do everything so there has to be some thinking about how to allocate the resources. Should the resources go into marketing? Should the resources go into improving the product? Should the resources go into training? How should you spend your income – on a new house or on the children's school fees?

There is a need to look into the future and the possible consequences of any decision. How are values going to be delivered? How are values going to be affected? When you look into the future, what are you going to be looking for? Changes in value are what you are going to be seeking, whether on a business or individual level.

TIMING

Then there is the choice of timing. Should we do something immediately? Should we do it soon? Should we do it later? Should we wait for things to change first? Can you do that without assessing values?

COST-CUTTING

Cost-cutting is a natural part of any review programme. The purpose is usually to reduce costs by eliminating functions and people who seem to be dispensable. On a personal level it can involve tightening your household budget or getting a better mortgage deal.

Again the process is one of looking into the consequences of any change and assessing values. In these cases there is a double value scan:

1   *To assess the value and the contribution of the function under review. Are the values high?*

 **11**

2   *To assess the value outcome if the change is made, if the function is closed down or outsourced.*

There is no natural law that states that things have to grow efficiently, so periodic review is essential. The same goes for complexity. Step by step, things may become ever more complex. So there is a need, periodically, to review matters in an effort to find a simpler way of doing things.

DESIGN

The whole purpose of design is to put things together 'to deliver value', so this is an obvious area in which close attention to values has to be paid.

> **Without a strong sense of value there is no design.**

A designer has to keep in mind the primary values to be delivered. This is the main purpose of the design. A car has to provide personal transport. Then there are the secondary values to be taken into consideration, such as price, comfort, prestige, looks, fuel consumption and re-sale price. Then there are the things to avoid or 'negative values' (see page 21), such as high cost of repair, poor environmental reputation, cheap image and difficulty in loading.

STRATEGY AND PLANS

You need to design a strategy and then decide whether to use it and when to use it.

Strategy which is not value driven is not a strategy at all.

What are we seeking to achieve? What must we try to avoid? How can the strategy be implemented? What are the values involved in the implementation? These values apply equally to business strategies and personal life plans.

START-UP

The design of any new business is a total exercise in value scanning. What are the values being offered to potential customers? What are the business values? Why would this business be profitable and durable?

Neglect of values led to the boom and bust of the 'dot com' phenomenon. The only value offered was that people would invest in dot com business because they could, almost immediately, sell on at a profit to other investors. This is exactly the same value that is offered in the illegal Ponzi (pyramid) schemes in which new investors are paid out of funds put in by previous investors.

The value scan may provide a go or no-go decision. More importantly, the value scan determines the design and modification of the start-up concept.

Making a decision to start something new on a personal level also involves this degree of value scanning. Whether it be a new relationship or a new job, the start of anything new in your life benefits from a thorough appraisal of your values.

DISPUTES

Disputes and conflicts usually arise because there is a clash of values. Each party in the dispute wants to pursue its own values – often at the expense of the other party.

Disputes can be solved by mediation, by arbitration or by law. There can be an attempt to discover and remove the cause of the dispute.

In all cases the best approach is to seek to design a way forward that benefits both parties. That requires a full understanding of the values of all parties involved in the dispute. Without such an understanding it is impossible to design an acceptable way forward.

Analysis and Values

The purpose of analysis is to understand the world around us so well that we can deliver and enjoy our values.

If you are hungry and your value is that you should eat, and if added social values make you want to eat out at a restaurant, then what is going to help you enjoy your values? A restaurant guide to the city will help you enjoy your values.

Our main thinking habit is to analyse situations so that we can recognise standard situations and then apply standard answers. This is an excellent system but there are dangers.

If circumstances have changed, then the standard answer may no longer be appropriate and may even be dangerous. So we need a value scan to assess whether the usual answer will be suitable in this particular instance.

So if you are hungry and want to eat out at a restaurant but you are saving hard to buy a house, your values have changed. You can go ahead and eat at a restaurant, but this will have a negative value on your bank balance, your plans and your family's future security.

Perception and Value

Values will direct and change our perception. At the same time, perception can change our values.

If you perceive someone to be a competitor then your evaluation of whatever that party does will be influenced by that perception.

If you perceive that someone was acting out of fear rather than aggression then your evaluation of the behaviour will be different.

Perception is rarely neutral unless driven by routine. Usually there is some value driving the perception. If you are hungry you perceive a sandwich in a different way from someone who is not hungry.

We may, therefore, need to do a value scan to see what values might be driving our perception.

In a way, a perception is an unconscious decision about how we see the world around us. Because it is unconscious we have no control over our perceptions unless we make the driving values visible.

Some people make the mistake of believing that we see things objectively first and then apply our values. Unfortunately, it is not like that. Values determine our perception, whether or not we are conscious of those values, and then what we see tends to support that perception.

Logic and Values

There are those who believe that decisions are made entirely by logic. You assemble the relevant information and then you apply your logic.

This does work, but only in a few cases. Suppose there is a mechanical breakdown. Logical analysis can lead you to the cause of the breakdown and you can then put it right.

Logic can help you decide how to do something but logic cannot tell you what you *want* to do.

Do you want to make more profits and return more to the shareholders or do you want to spend on developing a better marketing infrastructure? Do you want to accept a job promotion for more money or retrain for a career you would enjoy more? In the end your values will make that decision.

Logic can tell you that you could reduce the cost of a product by offering it in only one colour, like Henry Ford who famously remarked, 'Any customer can have a car painted any colour he wants so long as it is black.' At the same time, logic will tell you that in a competitive world, customers might not like this and might buy from your competitors. What are your values?

Logic is good at finding the best way to a destination. Logic may even appear to 'decide' on the destination. In the background, however, are the values that decide what you want to do.

Logic will tell you that you need to buy an overcoat in cold weather. Logic will tell you that a black overcoat will not show the dirt and is suitable for most occasions. But your values will decide whether you want the coat or not.

The real difficulty is that any decision made on a value basis can always be 'rationalised' in hindsight as having been made on a purely logical basis.

You like red wine. Then you rationalise it as healthy because red wine contains polyphenols which block an enzyme that permits fatty deposits in arteries and so reduces your chance of a heart attack. You may choose to ignore that the benefits apply only when red wine is consumed in moderation.

Now there might be people who genuinely choose red wine on that basis but there are others who use it to rationalise their choice. In any case, choosing red wine because it is good for you is a 'value' choice. Is your value to live a long time or to have fun in your life? Or to seek to do both?

There is no harm in rationalising decisions except for two things:

1 *We can seek to rationalise a bad decision made purely on an emotional basis. If we are good at rationalising we may not realise just how bad the decision really is.*
2 *If we come to believe our decisions are entirely logical, the greater danger is that we then neglect to pay attention to our values and may not even realise how they are affecting our 'logical' decisions.*

Values and Emotions

Are emotions the same as values? Values are the underlying drivers that bring about our emotions.

Someone insults you and you react emotionally. What is happening? What are the background values here?

Someone is acting aggressively towards you so you have to defend yourself. You do not want to be put down. You do not want to 'lose'. You do not want to be dominated (in a tribal sense).

You do not want others to see that you have been humiliated without a response.

There is the cultural value which suggests you should not accept being insulted.

There might be a slight dent to your self-image: maybe the insult is slightly right?

A completely different value set would suggest that you are not insulted unless you feel insulted. So instead of getting upset you just burst out laughing.

If your values are threatened your emotions indicate what you feel about that threat. The same applies to pleasure. When our values are provided we feel happy and may show our happiness.

Someone who is recognised and praised for having done a good job appreciates the recognition. The value involved is the social value of 'being noticed'.

2 ●●●●●●

NEGATIVE VALUES

Some people will not like the term 'negative value' because they will see it as a contradiction in terms. Could you have 'negative success' or 'negative goodness'?

However, there are certain things which cause harm and damage. Putting polluted water into a river causes ecological harm. Insulting someone can cause human relations harm.

Actions are almost as likely to have a negative effect (somewhere) as they are to have the intended positive effect.

Using words like 'harm' and 'damage' puts the negative aspects on a different scale from the positive aspects. Creating the term 'negative values' puts everything on the same scale so that everything can be considered at once.

Impact

Whatever the origin of the word 'value', we can broaden the meaning to indicate 'impact'. Whenever we do something there is likely to be an impact on other people or other things – and on ourselves.

We call this impact a value when the impact is positive. When it is negative we call the impact harm, damage or even cost.

The suggestion is that we enlarge the meaning of value to include any form of impact. If the impact is positive, then we use the ordinary word 'value' that has a positive flavour. If, however, we want to indicate that the impact is negative, then we use the term 'negative value'.

The term 'negative value' is very easy to understand, whatever language purists may feel. In any case, language has to grow and develop as circumstances change. Today there is more concern with the environment than ever before in history. We need a word which indicates a negative impact on the environment. That word, however, should be thought of at the same time as traditional values.

It would save time and transport costs to build the factory on the river. Those are important values. Another value is the supply of labour because people live on the river bank. The major negative value is the risk of polluting the river.

In this way, both types of value can be considered at the same time.

If we raise the price on these cosmetics, more people will regard them as a premium product. They will appreciate them as a premium product. They will appreciate them more and pay more for the product. The product will also probably do them more good if they consider it to be superior. I can see all those as values. The negative values are that some existing customers will simply not be able to afford to go on buying the product. Another negative value is that in the higher price range we shall be competing against the premium products with their marketing budgets. A possible negative value is that a few people will consider the price rise a 'rip-off'. They would want to know why we are raising prices. So there are both the values and the negative values.

Why not just use the word 'impact' and place 'positive' or 'negative' before it? The answer is that the word 'value' is so firmly established in culture and thinking that it would be very difficult to replace with a new word like 'impact'.

> With the suggestions put forward here, the word 'value' retains its full traditional use. Value means a 'positive impact'.

In addition, there is now the new term 'negative value' which in no way detracts from the usual sense of the world 'value'. In fact, the term 'negative value' enhances the understanding that values are automatically positive.

It is understandable that language has evolved to have different words for the positive and negative aspects of something. We have 'rude' as the negative aspect of 'polite'. But then we also have the word 'impolite'. That might mean just an absence of politeness or direct rudeness. So we could talk about 'unvalues' but this is much more cumbersome (and difficult to hear) than talking about 'negative values'.

Checking Values

We do not check values often enough because values seem vague. Values are important but it is difficult to focus on values. We *sort of know* what they are and that they are important, but we find it difficult to pay much attention to them.

A young man finds a particular young woman attractive. This is a fact. But the young man finds it difficult to explain why that young woman is attractive. In the same way we can decide that we 'like' something but find it difficult to spell out the values that drive that 'liking'.

The framework put forward in this book makes it easier to focus on values, easier to see values and easier to ask others about values.

3 ●●●●●●

FRAMEWORKS

Frameworks for directing attention are simple but can be very powerful in action. Without such frameworks, attention just drifts about or is 'pulled' only by apparently interesting items.

A framework for directing attention when we are considering values is given later in this book. Like the other frameworks described in this chapter, it is simple and powerful. There is nothing more effective than 'powerful simplicity'.

> **The framework given in this book is a framework for directing our attention to different sorts of values when we are assessing values.**

First let's look at some other frameworks we can use to direct our thinking.

Attention

Close your eyes. Wait one minute. Now open your eyes again. What do you see?

You see everything, or do you? There are no blind spots and you probably do not have a migraine which can greatly reduce your vision. Everything is as it was. Everything is as it should be. You know that. But do you see it?

Look straight ahead. Then direct your eyes about 20 degrees to your right. Now look up at the ceiling. Describe in detail what you see. You have probably never seen that detail before. You have indeed seen it as part of the 'whole scene' but seeing something as part of the whole scene is not the same as directing your attention to one specific area.

It is not possible to pay attention to everything at once. So what do we pay attention to?

We look out for important things. If you are driving a car you look out for traffic lights, for road signs, for pedestrians and for other traffic. These things are important because we know them to be important.

Your friends take you bird-watching and you see two birds prancing about. You are not sure what to look for until your friend advises you to look for the position of the male bird's head. You focus on this and suddenly the whole scene becomes more interesting.

Things that are important 'pull' our attention. Things that are interesting pull our attention. Things that we have been told to look out for pull our attention.

There is a huge difference between the word 'pull' and the word 'direct'.

Interesting things catch and hold our attention. A man wearing a bright pink suit would catch our attention. The word 'pull' implies that the object itself pulls our attention to that object.

In the exercise where you 'directed' your attention 20 degrees to the right and then to the ceiling, you were directing your attention yourself. There might have been nothing to see at all.

North, South, East and West

The points of the compass are important because they provide a framework we can use to 'direct' our attention. You can ask someone to 'look east'. You can ask someone to 'drive south'. You can describe the location of a house as being 'west of the church'.

'Right' and 'left' are similar direction frameworks. When you are about to cross a road a sign might say 'look right' to remind you to look at oncoming traffic. You are describing a painting to someone: 'To the right of the woman's head you can see the large coat of arms.'

Other People's Views

In the thinking programme I designed for schools there are specific 'attention-directing' tools. These function exactly like the compass points or like 'right and left'. You can instruct yourself, or someone else, to direct your attention in a specific way. For example, the OPV tool means 'direct your attention to the thinking of the other people involved: Other People's Views'.

Use of simple attention-directing tools like these reduced tribal fights in a mine in South Africa from over 200 fights a month to just four. In one example two drivers of underground locomotives were involved in a fight. One of them said to the other: 'Let's do an OPV.' The fight just dissolved. These thinking courses are now mandatory on the school curriculum in some countries. They are also used in industry.

Research by David Perkins at Harvard has shown that 90 per cent of the errors in thinking are errors of perception. If you see something incorrectly or inadequately, no matter how excellent your logic might be, the resulting action will be inappropriate.

> **The attention-directing tools serve to broaden and enrich perception. Instead of waiting for things to 'pull' our attention we can deliberately direct our attention as we wish and in a systematic way.**

The Six Thinking Hats

Argument is really a rather crude way of exploring a subject. Each side makes a case. Thereafter, one side seeks to defend its own case and to attack the other case. The other side does exactly the same.

If the prosecutor in a court of law sees a point which would help the defence case the prosecutor is never going to reveal such a point. If the defence lawyer sees a point which would help the prosecution case, the defence lawyer is certainly not going to bring that point up. There is case-making instead of exploration of the subject.

With the 'parallel thinking' of the Six Hats method, everyone directs their attention in the same way at every moment. Under the White Hat, for example, everyone focuses on information. What do we have? What is needed? What is missing? What questions should we ask?

Under the Black Hat everyone focuses on 'caution points'. What might go wrong? Why might it not fit our resources? Potential problems and weaknesses? This is the hat for critical thinking.

And so it goes for all six hats. In this way there is joint and objective exploration of the subject. Every person is doing his or her best to explore the subject objectively rather than just making a case.

The method is now widely used around the world across a very wide range of people: from four-year-olds in schools to top executives at corporations like

Siemens, Dupont and NTT. Meetings take from a quarter to a tenth of the usual time. The method gets the best thinking out of everyone. Corporations claim to have saved millions of pounds using this method.

> The Six Hats method is a framework for 'directing attention' and for doing one thing at a time.

The Six Action Shoes

I have also designed a framework for 'action'. This framework identifies the six major styles of action so you can identify which style (or combination of styles) is appropriate. This framework is the Six Action Shoes.

The action framework arose during a discussion with senior police officers. They complained that it was difficult to train a police officer to know what to do in a wide variety of situations, such as looking after a lost child, filing a report, pursuing an armed criminal, giving evidence in court, patrolling the streets, investigating domestic violence. The Action Shoes framework allows the trainer to identify the style of action – or combination of styles – required in any particular instance. The main value is that it allows the police officer himself or herself to identify the style of action needed 'right now'.

Perception

Can you see something for which there is no name? In the physical sense you can, of course, see that thing. But you may not 'notice' it and the thing may not register in your mind.

The corner of a table is simply the coming together of two edges. The word 'corner' is an adequate description but is not peculiar to tables. Suppose the corner of a table were given a special name: perhaps, 'anglent'. Now you might start noticing the anglent. Designers might start paying more attention to anglents. In time, anglents might become special features of a table and you might even identify the table designer from the anglents.

If you know that the top of a door is called a 'lintel' then you might start paying more attention to lintels in historic buildings. You can discuss lintels and be informed about lintels. All this is easier than talking about 'the top of the door'.

When a lot of people are together in a crowd they get excited. When they get excited they over-breathe. Such over-breathing washes the carbon dioxide out of the blood. The result is that the blood vessels in the brain tend to contract and less oxygen gets to the brain. This lack of oxygen lowers alertness and may result in a semi-hypnotic state. This means that crowds are easily swayed by leaders and the behaviour around them. If we had just one word for this 'pre-hypnotic stage of oxygen deprivation' then we would be more able to recognise this state and comment on it.

The expression 'cover your arse' is not very elegant but it is expressive. The expression allows us to notice, to comment upon and to describe a very specific type of behaviour: when you act to make sure that blame does not fall upon you.

The expression Nimby in politics means that you may be fully in favour of something which needs doing, like building a home for drug addicts, but you do not want it in your constituency: Not In My Back Yard. Giving a name to something allows us to recognise and deal with that something more effectively. The names given to values in this book enable us to notice such values, to look for them and act upon them.

Purpose

So the purpose of frameworks is twofold:

1   *Frameworks allow us to direct attention at will.*
    Frameworks allow us to ask others to direct their
    attention in a certain way. Attention no longer drifts
    from point to point. Attention is no longer pulled by
    items which seem interesting – at the expense of
    those items which are less interesting at first but, in
    the end, much more important.
2   *Frameworks allow us to give 'names' to things so that*
    we can look for them, look at them and notice them.

4 ●●●●●●

SIX VALUE MEDALS

Medals are an award to recognise special merit. In the Olympic Games, gold, silver and bronze medals are given to the winners of events. In many countries special medals are given for meritorious service.

The relationship between merit and medals is also clear in wartime when medals are given for valour and bravery.

Medals are not a reward in the sense that position or money could be an award. Medals are an acknowledgment of merit.

The Six Value Medals are an acknowledgment of merit. The merit is the level of value.

Symbol

Just as the 'hats' provide a perceptual symbol in the parallel thinking framework (see page 29), so the 'medals' provide a perceptual symbol in a value scan.

The symbol is used within our minds to help organise our thinking. When others come to know the framework then the symbol can also be used in communication:

What are the silver medal values here?

The sheer artificiality of the system is one of its greatest strengths. The new 'medal' symbols create a new 'game'.

Say you want to get someone to behave in a certain way. You could try persuasion but this lasts only a short time. Following persuasion, there may be a change in behaviour but this lasts only for a week unless there is something to 'anchor' the behaviour. The symbolism of the medals provides that 'anchor'.

Attitudes, no matter how wonderful, are very difficult to build up. That is why religions have so much symbolism. The rituals and symbols of religion serve to carry the attitudes and serve as constant reminders of the attitudes. You pick up the symbol and the attitude comes with it.

If you sit back in an armchair, removed from the real world, you might argue that creating new concepts and symbols is unnecessary. In the real world such symbols make a huge difference. That is why philosophy is so often removed from the real world.

In the old Marxist days in Bulgaria they started to teach my methods in schools. They asked one nine-year-old girl from the town of Plovdiv: 'Do you use these things you learn in the thinking lessons in real life?'

She replied: 'Oh yes, I use them all the time in real life. I even use them outside life, in school!'

Focus

You cannot look in all directions at once. That is why the compass directions help.

> If you ask someone to look for 'all values', this is quite a complex task. By separating out the different types of value we make the task possible. You now look in one direction at a time. This focusing aspect is important.

You can now ask for the exploration of one type of value at a time. This is much more specific and much more focused than asking for all values all the time.

Attention tends to drift and follow the easiest route at any moment – not unlike water flowing over a landscape. Having value categories prevents that drift. You stop yourself from drifting outside the category you are exploring at the moment. You are now conscious that you are crossing a boundary. You can also stop others from drifting in their exploration of values.

For all these reasons, the Six Value Medals framework has a lot of practical usefulness that is not easily seen until the method is put into practice.

Materials

Each of the six medals is 'made' of a different material. These materials have been chosen to provide a relevant metaphor. The material brings to mind an association between the medal and the values it indicates. The 'wood medal', for example, suggests nature, environment and ecology.

With frequent use, the term 'medal' may be dropped. So instead of asking for the 'silver medal values', you might come to ask for the 'silver values'.

Overview of the Six Value Medals

This is a quick overview of all the medals. Each medal will then get full attention in a chapter of its own.

GOLD MEDAL: This medal deals with **human values**, the values that affect people. Gold is a superior material and human values are the most important values of all in the end. What are the human values here?

SILVER MEDAL: This medal focuses directly on **organisational values**. That means values related to the purpose of the organisation (in business this would be profitability). Silver is associated with money. There are also the values involved in the actual running of the organisation, such as cost control. The organisation may also be a family, group of friends or social club.

STEEL MEDAL: These are the **quality values**. Steel should be strong. The values are in the intended direction. What are the values of the product, service or function in terms of what it is trying to do? If it is tea, is it good quality tea?

GLASS MEDALS: This medal covers a number of associated values: **innovation, simplicity and creativity**. Glass is a very simple material originating in sand. But with glass you can use your creativity to do a lot of things.

WOOD MEDAL: These are the **environmental values** in the broadest sense. What are the impact values on the environment, on the community, on others? The values relate to those things and people not directly involved.

BRASS MEDAL: This medal deals explicitly with **perceptual values**. How does this appear? How might it be seen? Perception is real even when it is not reality. Brass looks like gold.

Each of these medals will be considered in much more detail in subsequent chapters.

Imagine you were about to award a particular medal. You would look very closely at the values that were going to merit that award. It is exactly in this sense that the medals are used.

What are the brass medal values here?

GOLD MEDAL VALUES

Gold is very valuable. Gold does not tarnish. The winner in an Olympic event is given a gold medal. There is a certain hierarchy among the medals with gold being the most valuable. This is hardly surprising because, in the end, human values must come first.

> **Without human values there is exploitation, slavery and tyranny. The whole purpose of civilisation is a combined effort to attend to human values.**

Assessing Gold Medal Values

When we set out to assess gold medal values we can look at the possible effects of a proposed change, or we can review the existing situation.

Gold Medal Values of a Change

There is a proposed change or a new project. What will the impact be on human values?

How will this affect gold medal values?
Have you considered the gold medal values?
I suspect this is going to have a major gold medal impact.

In organisations, the impact of any change on profits or operations is always considered. In our personal lives, we also tend to look closely at the financial impact of any change. If the impact is negative in either situation, the change does not go ahead. The impact on human values is probably not considered so fully. If there are compelling economic reasons for doing something then negative gold medal values (like laying people off) will not stop the change. After all, if the organisation ceases to exist, everyone will be out of a job.

Similarly, we may decide to move to a different part of the country to take up a lucrative job offer. The negative human values here are leaving behind friends and family.

If survival is a priority value then it may over-ride other values.

Gold Medal Values of an Existing Situation

In a review situation, an assessment is made of existing gold medal values. There may be deficiencies. There may be room for improvement. There may be new suggestions.

For example, an organisation may review its provision for maternity leave. This is a strong human value. The company may be prompted to be more generous in order to retain female executives. On a personal level, you may review the gold medal values of your family life. Is there enough time in your schedule to devote to your partner or children?

The Range of Human Values

There is a huge range of human values. The ones listed here are only suggestions, and you are invited to add further to the list in the space provided (see page 47). Your own experience, your own special circumstances, your own values may suggest additional ones.

Basic Needs

The widely accepted basic needs of human beings include food, shelter, health and respect.

Earning a fair wage enables us to provide for most of these basic needs. Our tax system provides healthcare services and the welfare state aims to cover the basic needs of those who do not earn enough to meet their own needs.

HEALTH

There are two aspects to health:

1 *Is there anything in the workplace that might negatively impact health? This would need attention and correction.*
2 *General health. This may involve clinics, medical services, counselling and testing. Assistance in providing access to outside medical services would also help.*

SHELTER

Shelter means affordable housing. This could mean provision of low-cost housing, assistance with mort-gages and transport to less expensive living areas. In many areas of London, public service employees sim-ply cannot afford to buy a house within reasonable distance of where they work.

RESPECT

Respect is a broad word which covers the way you are treated by others. This includes dignity. It includes lack of discrimination. It may include 'belonging'. It always includes absence of bullying and oppression of any sort. It includes a concept of 'fair treatment'. Organisations and educational institutions sometimes produce a charter in which they display their commitment to treating staff and students with respect. Informal rules of respect can be brought into play within a family, where everyone is aware of how others should be treated. Many of these aspects will also be considered later.

Freedom From . . .

There will be a lot of 'negative values' in the gold medal area. Freedom from these negative values then becomes a value.

> Freedom from **tyranny, oppression and bullying** is a very high value. The life of a child at school or a worker in a factory may be made intolerable by bullying.

Schools try to address bullying by making pupils aware of strategies they can use if they are bullied. It is essential that children can access adult support without fear of the bullying getting worse.

Freedom from **discrimination and unfairness** is of major importance. Human beings are very sensitive to 'unfairness'. It is true that sometimes the label of discrimination can be applied to things which are not that at all. A general feeling of unfairness may be more important than an individual feeling.

It is very important that employers do not discriminate on grounds of gender or race. It is essential that employees have someone to talk to within their organisation about any instances of discrimination.

Freedom from **anxiety and uncertainty** is another value. This value is, however, more difficult to achieve. It is true that life is uncertain for everyone. It is true that it is not possible to protect people from uncertainty because the world is a changing place that generates uncertainty.

Freedom from **violence** is essential. This may not be outright physical violence. There may be psychological violence. This value also covers sexual harassment.

Freedom from **stress and pressures** is necessary. If people work hard out of motivation then pressure may not be required.

Psychological Needs

In practice, these may be even more important than the other needs, because the other needs have already been considered and taken care of.

Recognition is a broad need and an important one. This means that a person is 'noticed' and given attention. The very existence of that person is acknowledged. Children benefit from being given a special sticker for good work or being praised in assembly for a sporting or musical achievement.

When workers in the research department of a major corporation were asked what rewards they wanted for their discoveries and inventions, they replied 'recognition'. They wanted senior management to recognise what they had done.

Appreciation and thanks are part of recognition. It may be felt that appreciation and thanks are only given for special efforts. There is no reason why they should not be given more widely. At the same time, some research claims to show that if a child in school is praised for everything, learning can be affected negatively.

Prestige and 'importance' matter to some people. There may be ways of making this possible with 'employee of the month' awards and similar schemes.

Simplicity is a human value. People become stressed if procedures are too complex. Mistakes are made with complex tasks, and people do not like making mistakes or being blamed for making them.

Trust is a key value. Do workers trust management? Do people trust the government? Do wives trust their husbands? Do children trust their teachers?

Reassurance is a value. People need to know if they are doing well.

Encouragement is a value. If someone seems to believe in you, then you try harder. Incentive schemes leading to bonuses can greatly encourage employees to achieve their potential. Children respond well to star charts that award them a star for a desired behaviour and a treat when a certain number of stars have been earned.

A sense of achievement is highly important to everyone. So creating the possibility of visible 'achievement' is important. Having a small celebration or treat when a child achieves something important can be very valuable. Indeed, adults should take time to celebrate their achievements as well.

People need **help** from time to time. Being able to provide or to organise such help is a value.

Simple human warmth is another value that is easier in small organisations than in larger ones. Warmth is the next stage on from 'respect'. We can show warmth to our family, friends and neighbours.

Human dignity is another major value, particularly when it is degraded. Respect is of importance here. There is respect for a person as another human being. There is respect for a person as a particular human being.

We need the value of **hope** to give us the incentive to carry on. At work, this may be the hope of promotion or a pay rise. On a personal level, this may be the hope that we will find love or have children.

What Are Your Gold Medal Values?

My own listing is offered only as an example of what can be included under gold medal values. You are invited to add further to this list with notes in the space given here. There may be important points that I have left out. You may wish to express differently some of the points I have mentioned. There may be special circumstances or special cultures that demand the inclusion of further values.

ADDITIONAL GOLD MEDAL VALUES:

_____

_____

_____

_____

_____

_____

_____

_____

_____

_____

_____

_____

_____

_____

_____

_____

_____

_____

_____

_____

Summary

1 Gold medal values are specifically concerned with human values. What are the values that matter to individuals, both as human beings and also in certain circumstances? How are people being treated? What is the likely impact on human values of changes? What is the existing state of gold medal values?

2 There are many 'negative values' in this area. Very often the removal or prevention of such negative values is an important value in itself.

3 There are basic human needs. Then there is the need to be free from negative values. There are a lot of psychological values which affect the way people feel – and the way they work and contribute.

4 When you are looking at gold medal values you focus on these human values.

SILVER MEDAL VALUES

These are the direct 'organisation values'. In general, the silver medal values are those organisation values that are not included under the gold medal values.

There is an overlap between the gold and silver value medals in the sense that if workers are not happy and do not work well, this affects the profitability of a corporation. So, in a sense, the unhappiness of the workers becomes an organisation value.

In a complex organisation everything affects everything else. A family or social group can also be seen as an organisation. Silver medal values apply just as much to these groups as to businesses.

You could say that one of the elements of the silver medal values is 'to get the gold medal values right'.

There are two broad types of silver medal values:

1   *How well the organisation is achieving its chosen
    and intended purpose.*
2   *How well the organisation is running.*

Using a car analogy, the first values relate to whether
the car is on course for the chosen destination. The
second values relate to how well the car is actually
running.

Purpose

What is the purpose of a business corporation?

- *The purpose may be to sell goods or services at a profit.*
- *The purpose may be to maximise the return to
  shareholders.*
- *The purpose may be to contribute to society by
  providing needed goods or services.*
- *The purpose may be to provide employment to all the
  people working in the corporation.*
- *The purpose may be to continue to exist and to survive.*

You could add to this list of purposes. The two key elements might be: to survive; to maximise. What is the
mechanism by which this is going to be achieved? By
selling desired goods and services at a profit.

There is no need to seek to be profound or philosoph-
ical about a definition of purpose. The purpose of most
corporations is to sell goods and services at a profit.

This definition of purpose will then include several silver medal values:

- *The goods or services have to be **produced** or **organised**.*
- *The goods or services have to be **saleable** in terms of being attractive to customers – otherwise there are no sales. This covers the values of research, product design, product change and market research.*
- *The **pricing** of the goods and services has to be right both from a competitive point of view and in terms of profitability. You would not want to be selling goods at below cost. If, however, the price is too high you may not sell very much.*
- *Then there is the whole matter of **distribution**. How do the goods and services get to the customer? Is the distribution through shops, agencies or the internet?*
- *How do people get to know about your product or service and why it may be better than a competitor's? Through **advertising**, **public relations** and **promotions**.*

In the end, silver medal values contribute to revenue and profits. There may be fewer sales at a higher price. There may be high-volume sales at a lower price. Profitability is the key issue.

From the point of view of the stock market, the returns to shareholders may be the key purpose of any corporation.

All these, and many more, are silver medal values with regard to the purpose of an organisation.

Different Organisations, Different Purposes

With different organisations the 'purpose' type of silver medal values might change.

For a political party the purpose might be achieving more votes and getting elected to government. Anything that helps with this is a silver medal value. Anything that obstructs the process is a negative silver medal value.

The purpose for a charitable foundation is to find and support worthwhile causes. There is also the visibility side – the charity may want to be seen to be doing good. Where the charity is involved in raising new funds then the silver medal values may refer to success in fundraising.

Forming this alliance will increase our public profile and help us to raise more funds.

For a government the purpose may be to satisfy the electorate and to show that things are being done. To keep the electorate supportive is the key purpose value.

The purpose silver medal values for a public service might be to provide a smooth service, to reduce complaints and to simplify procedures.

For a restaurant the purpose values might be to serve more meals profitably and to get a good reputation that ensures custom.

Silver medal values within a family could relate to household finances. The purpose of the family is not financial in itself, but money is necessary for the family to survive.

Operations

The other set of silver medal values applies to the functioning of the organisation:

- *Is there good cost control in place?*
- *How efficient is the production process? Would outsourcing be an option?*
- *Do we have the right organisational structure in place?*
- *Recruiting the right people is important. Retaining people may also be important.*
- *Communication between departments and sectors is a high value. I once heard of a major corporation which paid a firm of consultants $24 million a year just to get the different departments to talk to each other.*
- *How good are the accounting procedures that are in place? Can they prevent the sort of major disasters that happen from time to time with corporations?*

Levels

Silver medal values apply at all levels within an organisation.

The efficient allocation of lecture halls in a university is a silver medal concern. So is the availability of lecturers. The quality of the lectures may be both a silver medal concern and a steel medal concern (see Chapter 7). Parking spaces for workers and the efficiency of the cafeteria are also silver medal concerns.

At every level there are concerns with how to make things run more smoothly and more efficiently. In a family these values are also very important. Parents of primary school children need to ensure the children are delivered to school and collected on time, that they are prompt for any extracurricular activities and that all homework, sports kit and dinner money is present and correct.

In many cases 'effectiveness' is even more important than efficiency. Is the operation effective? Is the organisation effective? Cost considerations then bring in the need for efficiency as well.

Problem-Solving

As with gold medal values, there are silver medal values concerned with removing 'negative values'. The removal of negative values is always a positive value (see Chapter 1).

There is a problem with 'just in time' delivery. There is a problem with warehouse capacity. There is a problem with IT flexibility. There is a problem with excess noise on the shop floor. There is a hold-up on the production line.

In the family there is a problem with finding childcare. There is a problem with a DIY project. There is a mix-up with the holiday booking.

Problems, deficiencies and inefficiencies all provide negative silver medal values. Putting these things right provides silver medal values.

Putting in a new machine that improves production could be seen as coming under the silver medal but also under the steel medal which is concerned with 'quality' (see Chapter 7).

Innovations and simplifications within the organisation could come under the silver medal but also under the glass medal which deals with innovation (see Chapter 8).

There is no difficulty with this overlap. A ceramic ornament could be looked at both as a ceramic work and also as an ornament. An employee could be looked at both as an employee and also as a parent.

What Are Your Silver Medal Values?

As with the gold medal, you are invited to add your own further examples of silver medal values. These could fall either under 'purpose' values or 'operational' values.

There may be values which are particular to your organisation, family or group. There may be values you know from experience to be key values.

ADDITIONAL SILVER MEDAL VALUES:

_____

_____

_____

_____

_____

_____

_____

_____

_____

_____

_____

_____

_____

_____

_____

_____

_____

_____

_____

_____

Summary

1   Silver medal values are organisation values.
    These are values that arise from the intended
    purpose of the organisation. Those things
    that help the organisation fulfil its mission
    are silver medal values.

2   For different organisations there may be
    different silver medal purpose values, such
    as profits, votes and publicity.

3   Then there are the silver medal values
    concerned with the internal running of the
    organisation, such as cost control, efficiency,
    effectiveness and communication. In this
    area there may be a lot of negative silver
    medal values. There may be obstacles,
    problems and inadequacies. Removing these
    difficulties results in silver medal values.

4   Where there seems to be an overlap with
    other medal values, it becomes possible to
    look at the same thing in two ways. You may
    do both or choose one or the other.

7

STEEL MEDAL VALUES

Steel should be strong. Sugar should be sweet. A communication should be understandable. A package should protect. A headache cure should cure headaches. A love potion should do what a love potion should do.

> Steel medal values are directly concerned with quality. What are the quality values? What are the values that would help improve quality?

Customer Values

A customer buys a jacket. What are the 'jacket values'? The purchase values might include the price, the choice, the service in the store and the accessibility of the store. The quality of the jacket resides in the jacket.

There is the quality of the material. Is it warm? Is it hard-wearing?

There is the quality of appearance. Is it in fashion? Is the cut right? Does it fit me? Is the colour right? Is the style right for me?

There is the quality of the production. Is the sewing neat and unobtrusive? Is the lining properly fitted?

All these qualities are to do with the jacket and the relationship of the jacket to the purchaser. These values have nothing to do with the profitability of the organisation producing the jacket. They have nothing to do with how the workers in the factory are treated.

Quality of Service

In a restaurant you expect quality of food and quality of service. The service should be fast and efficient and not make mistakes. The service should be courteous and not intrusive. If the diner wishes to engage in conversation with the staff then the interchange should be handled with charm.

From the point of view of a taxpayer the tax system should have steel medal values. The tax demands must be simple, clear and unambiguous. There should be no confusion at all and no possibility of misinterpretation.

From the point of view of the government the operation of the tax system involves silver medal values. What is the cost of collecting every penny of tax? Does the system work smoothly? Are there complaints? The steel medal values – the taxpayers' point of view – needs to be taken into account in designing the system.

Parents seek quality when it comes to childcare. It is very important that their children are being cared for properly. Nurseries and childminders have silver medal values to consider – how much they will earn from providing the service – but they know the importance of steel medal values in what they do.

The quality of service in banks can, in my personal experience, be truly appalling. There can be a dangerous disregard for arrangements made with a customer and no consideration for the long-term loyalty of a customer. In some countries this has been partly due to the removal of functions from a local branch to a central office that has no knowledge of customers and cares very little for them.

Quite often there is a direct conflict between silver medal values and steel medal values. To cut costs (silver medal), services are reduced or centralised. The result is that the 'quality' reaching the customer (steel medal) is greatly reduced. Successful organisations seek a balance between silver and steel medal values. Reducing the quality of a service or product will have long-term repercussions on customer loyalty.

Function Quality

The horn in a car should have excellent function quality. It needs to be loud enough to warn other motorists but not so loud as to upset the whole street. Car horns probably should have three levels of volume. There could be a very loud horn for real danger. Then there could be a loud horn to alert other traffic to what is happening. Then there could be a gentle or polite horn to warn pedestrians. If pedestrians are walking in the middle of the street and a car wishes to get past, there needs to be something more 'polite' than a loud hoot.

A door latch needs to function efficiently. So does a toilet flushing system. Mobile phone access and operations need to be of top quality. Computer screens and keyboards need quality of function. Voice recognition software needs to offer consistent quality.

Quality implies that anything being done can probably be done better. Improvement and quality go together. The quality of meetings can be improved to give a quicker and more effective outcome. US managers spend up to 40 per cent of their time in meetings. Parallel thinking (Six Hats) is a powerful way of improving the quality of meetings.

Quality and Change

The function of a pen is to write. Quality improvements can be made in the grip of the pen, in the quality of the ink, in the delivery of the ink and perhaps in the aesthetics of the pen. The pen can also be designed to be 'expensive' and to indicate prestige (so making it a suitable gift item). If someone now adds the function of 'recording brief messages' on the pen, is this an improvement in quality?

On the one hand, there is an improvement in the quality of usefulness of the pen. On the other hand, the addition of the recording facility has not improved the basic quality of the pen as a writing instrument.

This sort of creative change would come under the 'glass medal values' (see Chapter 8). It is important to confine steel medal values directly to quality improvements. If we are always making 'innovative' changes we might never focus on direct quality improvements.

Sometimes it is possible that improvements in the same direction cannot go any further. When young Fosbury invented the 'Fosbury flop' in the high jump, his intention was to keep his rear end from hitting the crossbar. This was such an improvement that the Fosbury flop has been the method of high-jumpers ever since. The older methods simply cannot compete.

All improvement requires an element of change. Such change can be small or big enough to qualify as a creative change. Both directions need to be considered: small incremental changes and the big creative leap.

Negative Values

There can be problems and obstacles to quality improvements. Such negative values are probably less

to do with the steel medal than with the gold and silver medals (see Chapters 5 and 6).

A perceived problem is often welcomed as a starting point for quality improvement. If all organisations have the same problem, then overcoming that problem is a good opportunity to move ahead.

Actions elsewhere, however, can produce negative steel medal values. For example, a school might reduce the hours of a classroom assistant to save money (silver medal values) at the expense of the quality of teaching (steel medal values).

It is possible that a concern with the environment (wood medal values, see Chapter 9) might lead to a change in the material used with a decrease in quality (steel medal values).

Perceived Values

You see a simple wooden box. You do not know that it is made from a very rare wood. You do not know that this wood is very hard to work and that many hours of skilled craftsmanship have gone into the making of this box. In this case your perceived values are very different from the real values.

In general, it is the perceived quality of a product or service that matters to the customer. Tanzanite should be a very precious stone since it is mined only in one area of the world. The rarity value should be higher than that of a diamond. In perception, however, it is seen as a lesser gemstone.

Perceived values as such come under the brass medal (see Chapter 10). With the delivery of quality, however, there may be a need to communicate the true quality of what is being delivered.

Quality Focus

The steel medal values fit in well with the great attention quality has been getting for some time now. Programmes like 'Total Quality Management' seek to focus attention on steel medal values and provide frameworks for delivering these values. Most organisations are now conscious of the importance of quality. There is a slight danger, however, that if 'quality' as a term is enlarged to cover all operations and needs in an organisation, then the specific focus on 'quality' described here may be diluted.

It is similar to the use of the term 'critical thinking' to cover all thinking. The term then loses its ability to convey its original meaning which is 'judgment thinking'.

Parents are exhorted to spend 'quality time' with their children. This is a good use of the term 'quality' because not all uses of time are of high quality. If parents and children simply sit in the same room while everyone watches television, the quality of that time may not be high. More interaction with the children would be a more 'quality' use of time.

What Are Your Steel Medal Values?

As with the previous medals you are invited to add your own steel medal values to the ones I have mentioned here. Such additions may include your own interpretation of the term 'quality'. What do you think should also come under the steel medal value focus?

ADDITIONAL STEEL MEDAL VALUES:

Summary

1   Steel medal values are to do with quality. A product, service or function is designed to do something. Quality is the excellence with which something achieves what it sets out to do.

2   Customer values come under the steel medal. This covers products and services. The values the customer perceives are what is received by the customer. If such perceived values are less than the true values then there is a need for communication.

3   Improvement comes under the steel medal values. Improvement may be step by step and incremental or there may be a creative jump. It is important not to neglect small-step improvement in favour of the creative jump. Both tracks need to be followed.

4   Sometimes there is a conflict of values. Pursuit of other values can harm or reduce the steel medal values. For example, cutting costs may hurt customer value.

5   The existing focus on quality in organisations fits in well with the steel medal values.

8

GLASS MEDAL VALUES

There is something very special about glass as a material:

- *It is made out of sand and the end product bears no relationship to the original ingredients.*
- *Glass is relatively cheap as a material.*
- *Glass is usually clear and transparent.*

From this basic material, creativity can fashion amazing objects. In Venice, Italy, I have an island right next to Murano which is one of the most famous places in the world for beautiful glass. The owners of the oldest glass studio in the world, Barovier and Toso, are friends of mine. This enterprise has been running continuously since 1295.

> **Glass medal values are concerned with creativity, innovation and simplicity. These values apply in all areas. Anything we do and anything we think about can possibly be improved through creative thinking.**

Acting as a self-organising information system, the neural network of the brain allows information to form itself into patterns. These patterns are largely dependent on the sequence in which the information arrives.

We should be immensely grateful for these patterns because without them life would be impossible. With 11 items of clothing there are, theoretically, 39,916,800 ways of getting dressed. If you tried one way every minute of your waking life, you would need to live to 76 years of age to try them all.

Because of the excellence of the brain in forming routine patterns, we just identify the relevant patterns – the 'getting dressed pattern' – and get dressed in normal time.

This wonderful pattern-forming ability of the brain (described in my book *The Mechanism of Mind*, 1969) makes life possible but makes creativity difficult.

We have always treated creativity as a mystical gift or a special talent. This may apply to artistic creativity but not to the creativity of 'ideas'.

I gave the name 'lateral thinking' to thinking that moves across patterns rather than along them. There are formal techniques that can be learned and used. Using just one of these techniques, a group of workshops generated 21,000 ideas for a corporation in an afternoon. The methods are now widely used in corporations around the world.

Innovation

Innovation implies change and doing something differently. Innovation means putting into practice a new idea.

The new idea may have been generated through lateral thinking. The new idea may have been copied from someone else. The new idea may have been arrived at through logical analysis. The main point is that the idea is new for the organisation or individual implementing the idea.

If the idea has been shown to work elsewhere the risk may be low. If the idea is totally new the risk will be higher.

The glass medal values are the potential values arising from implementing the idea.

Glass medal values also arise from the habit of innovation and structures set up to encourage that habit. The spirit of innovation has its own glass medal values in addition to those arising from a particular innovation.

Simplicity

Simplicity is an important value. Over time things become more and more complex through additions without restructuring. There is no natural tendency towards simplicity. We have to make a deliberate effort to find a simpler way of doing things.

Simplicity can save time and money. Simplicity can reduce anxiety and mistakes. Simpler things are easier to put right. Simpler things are easier to learn and to maintain. That is why I once wrote a book called *Simplicity*.

The values arising from simplicity are glass medal values. Complexity and the absence of simplicity are negative glass medal values.

Simplicity itself must be regarded as a value so that everyone is always trying to simplify things. Creativity and lateral thinking can be used to find simpler ways of doing things.

Creativity

This refers to the actual generation of new ideas. These may be triggered by chance. They may be triggered by a chance coming-together of different things. Some people have developed creative attitudes and creative skills. There are traditional processes like brainstorming, which are in the right direction though rather weak in operation. There are the formal and deliberate tools of lateral thinking which can be learned and used.

All valued new ideas will always be logical in hindsight. If they were not logical in hindsight we would not be able to appreciate them – they would be crazy ideas. Because a new idea will be logical once created, we have claimed (for 2,400 years) that creativity is not needed and that better logic would have produced the idea.

This totally false idea is based on a lack of understanding of self-organising information systems that create asymmetric patterns. You cannot access the pattern but if, somehow, you reach the end of the road then you can easily find your way back.

It is this new 'logical' approach to creativity that makes lateral thinking so powerful. You no longer have to wait for inspiration.

The Culture of Creativity

Whether or not creativity happens within an organisations depends on the culture of that organisation – and this is usually set by the most senior level.

Many organisations have an unexpressed motto: 'Do not risk innovating but be quick to follow someone else's innovation when it has proved successful'. There is not much wrong with this 'me-too' strategy except that in many cases the first into the field remains the leader.

Those who fear creativity do so for two reasons:

1   *Any innovation has a risk factor and no one wants to be blamed for 'making a mistake'. No one is ever blamed for not developing an opportunity.*
2   *If everyone is trying to be creative then they will 'take their eye off the ball' and neglect the routines they*

should be using. Also, there would be chaos if
everything was being changed all the time.

These are, of course, extreme exaggerations.

It is important to emphasise that glass medal values apply in two ways. The first is the general value of innovation. The second is the specific value or benefit from a proposed idea.

Too often, creative people believe it is enough to have a creative idea. That is the fun of creation. Let other people assess and use the idea. The weakness of this approach is that 'novelty' as such is not necessarily attractive to other people. The creator of an idea should make a serious effort to show the glass medal values of the idea. Benefits, rather than novelty, persuade other people to explore and use the new idea.

Fragility

Glass is fragile and easily broken. There is a relevant metaphor here. New ideas are fragile and need nurturing. If an idea is subject to fierce attack as soon as the idea emerges then creativity is going to be difficult.

Before any new idea is put into serious use, the idea must show potential benefits that exceed the risk factor. So, at that final stage, judgment can be harsh. But before that stage there is a constructive effort to develop and to improve the idea.

Ways of pre-testing an idea also need to be designed. Ideas are much more likely to be accepted if a 'pre-test' has been designed into the idea in the first place.

Potential

Let's have some glass medal thinking here. What values could a new idea deliver at this point? What do we see as potential?

There is a huge difference between analysis and potential. You can analyse the past but you have to design the future. You need to open up possibilities and then design a way of making those possibilities into realities.

The readiness to be creative and creative effort are what matters.

If you reward creative effort you will get creative results. If you reward creative results you will not get creative effort.

The reason is that everyone is capable of creative effort but not everyone believes that he or she is capable of creative results.

What Are Your Glass Medal Values?

As in previous chapters, you can add your own glass medal values to my list.

The Six Value Medals

ADDITIONAL GLASS MEDAL VALUES:

_____

_____

_____

_____

_____

_____

_____

_____

_____

_____

_____

_____

_____

_____

_____

_____

_____

_____

_____

Summary

1   Glass medal values arise from innovation, creativity and simplicity. The values are concerned with values that arise from change.

2   There is evolutionary change; there is logical progression; there is change brought about by pressure; and there is deliberate creative change.

3   There are two aspects of glass medal values. There are the values that arise from a culture and spirit of creativity within an organisation. People take more interest in what they are doing as they seek improvements. Then there are the values that arise from the new idea.

4   Creative people should be encouraged to spell out the values and benefits of their ideas. It is not enough just to present novelty.

5   Glass medal values are very much concerned with 'potential' and imagining 'what might be'. This is different from an analysis of the past.

9 ●●●●●●

WOOD MEDAL VALUES

Wood medal values are to do with the environment in its broadest sense. The choice of 'wood' for this medal has some metaphorical relevance.

Wood is a natural substance which suggests 'nature'. Wood is a complex structure which also suggests that the environment is a complex matter.

Impact

> In the broadest sense, the wood medal values assess the impact of a decision, project, activity or change on 'third parties'. These third parties are not directly involved in the operation but are affected by it.

If you use your mobile phone in a cinema, all the people around you are affected and distracted, even though they are not at all involved in your conversation.

If you park your car in a busy street where you are not supposed to park, all other traffic passing through that street may be affected by your action, even though they are not involved.

If you pour a pollutant into a river then the living creatures in the river will be affected, as will all those people downstream who need to use the water.

The words 'selfish' and 'self-centred' imply that you are concerned only with your own interests. Wood medal values are exactly the opposite. Wood medal values ask for a consideration of all those affected by your behaviour – other than yourself and your interests.

Many people misunderstand the nature of 'manners'. These people believe that manners are the way you show respect to your friends and acquaintances. In fact, manners are exactly the opposite. Manners are the way you show respect to people who are not your friends at all! It is natural to treat your friends well. No special effort is required there. It is precisely the effort to treat strangers well that is the origin of manners. In exactly the same way, wood medal values involve a consideration of areas outside your own interests.

Nature

Because of increased environmental awareness and various protest groups (and legal actions), most people think of 'environment' as meaning 'the world of

nature'. There is no harm in this since the impact of industrialised society on nature can be very damaging. The pollution emitted by motor cars, the greenhouse gases emitted by factories that enlarge the 'ozone hole', the pollution of rivers and the sea are all of major concern.

In addition to the gases produced by industry, millions of tons of methane are produced by cattle and millions of tons of carbon dioxide are produced by termites.

Children in school are taught to be environmentally aware. They are taught wood medal values from an early age.

Various agreements and treaties have been attempted to try to control and regulate the emission of environmentally harmful gases.

A useful motto of the environment activists is 'Think globally and act locally'.

Every organisation needs to be conscious of its own impact on the local environment. In the family, it is important to consider how much household waste is produced. Could you purchase products with less packaging? How much household waste can be recycled?

If strip mining ravages the environment, how can this be repaired?

If offshore oil spills threaten marine life, how can this be prevented and limited?

Many organisations wait for pressure to be put on them by environmental groups, governments or legal actions. Then they respond to these pressures as best they can. This passive approach may no longer be enough. There is a growing need for organisations to do their own 'wood medal thinking' and to consider the environmental impact of their actions.

In some parts of the world 'environmental impact studies' are required before a project goes ahead. This is usually an external operation. There is an equal need for it to be internal.

Not surprisingly, there are often conflicts between the silver medal values (organisational, Chapter 6) and the wood medal values. Taking care of the wood medal values may be expensive and may limit operations.

Other Parties

Because 'environment' is so strongly associated with the natural environment, there is a tendency to ignore other 'impacts'.

Setting up a military base may encourage prostitution in nearby villages.

Establishing a factory in a rural area may drain limited labour resources from agriculture.

Pulling out of a town centre may hasten the decline in that part of town.

Outsourcing production to China may remove the major employment of a region.

The difficult question is the extent to which organisations should take these factors into account in their plan. Should they keep production where it is and lose out to their competitors? Should they remain in the town centre where profitability has fallen below all other sites? Do corporations have a social responsibility, and, if so, to what extent? Should governments provide 'social subsidies' to compensate for silver medal losses?

It is not the purpose of this book to tell people and organisations how to act on their values. The purpose is to make it easier for people to 'think' about their values. So wood medal thinking seeks to clarify the 'impact' value on others. What you do about the values, once you see them, is up to corporate ethics and strategy and, on a personal level, individual choice. If the final decision is not swayed by consciousness of these values, then mitigating action may be put in place to lessen their impact.

When a coal mine has to close, how can new employment opportunities be created for the miners who lose their jobs?

Competitors

In a sense competitors are 'third parties' that are impacted by an action or strategy. The possible impact on competitors may be assessed under the silver medal (Chapter 6) or under the wood medal.

How will competitors respond? Might the competitors start a price war, so wiping out the profitability for everyone? Might competitors respond with an immediate 'me-too', so reducing any advantage from the innovation?

Suppliers

It may be argued that suppliers are not really third parties but, like unions, are an integral part of the operation and so need to be considered under silver medal values (Chapter 6). This is a valid point, and you could consider suppliers under either, or both, medals.

If you change from one supplier to another, what impact will that have? Should you care?

Should you work with your suppliers to help them deliver the quality and price you require? Or should you keep them at arm's length and just choose the most suitable? Is supplier loyalty important?

Friends and Family

Decisions you make in your personal life are likely to have an impact on third parties, namely your friends and family. Major changes, such as moving abroad, have a strong effect on all those close to you. Even minor changes, like going on a diet, can affect those around you. Will your family have to eat the same foods as you? Will your friends have to put up with hearing about every pound you lose?

Negative Values

As was the case with gold medal values (Chapter 5), many of the wood medal values are negative. You need to be aware of these negative values. Once awareness is there you can choose various courses of action.

You can choose to avoid the negative values.

You can choose to reduce the negative impact.
You can choose to mitigate the negative impact.
You can choose to compensate for the negative impact.
You can choose to ignore them.
You can choose to assign them a low priority.

Once a thought is thought it cannot be unthought. Once a value is seen it cannot be unseen.

You may suggest that you would be better off not knowing about the negative values because then you would not need to do anything about them. This is like not going for a checkup in case the doctor finds something wrong with you.

If you do not want to keep good accounts, that is your business. If you do not want to follow regulations, that is your business. If you do not want to assess the values involved, that is your business. But if

you do want to lay out the values for your consideration then the wood medal is part of that exploration.

What Are Your Wood Medal Values?

As in earlier chapters you can now add further wood
medal values.

ADDITIONAL WOOD MEDAL VALUES:

_____

_____

_____

_____

_____

_____

_____

_____

_____

_____

_____

_____

_____

_____

_____

_____

_____

_____

Summary

1   Wood medal values explore the impact of your actions on third parties that are not directly involved. There is a need to consider these impact values.

2   There may be a major impact on the natural environment. This may be a local effect, such as polluting a river, or a contribution to a global effect, as in greenhouse gas emission.

3   There may be a social impact on a region. There may be a cultural impact.

4   Few things happen in isolation so the impact on other parties may be complex.

5   Wood medal values are often negative values. There is a need to prevent harm, to put it right or to mitigate it.

6   The role of wood medal thinking is to lay out the impact values involved. What you choose to do about them is up to you.

10 ●●●●●●

BRASS MEDAL VALUES

Perception is far more important than most people think. There is the belief that everyone can see the 'truth'. There is the belief that everyone can see things as they really are. Brass, however, can be perceived as gold.

> The brass medal is all about 'perceptual values'.
> *How does this look?*
> *How will this be seen?*
> *How else might it be seen?*

There is the belief that any tampering with perception is deceit or cheating. If the tampering is not that bad then it may just be 'cosmetic'.

Unfortunately, all these beliefs are totally wrong. People react to 'what they see', not the underlying reality. How could it be otherwise?

Perception is real even when it is not reality.

People are being fooled all the time. Occasionally,

this is deliberate deception. Occasionally, an over-enthusiastic salesperson leads people into purchases they should not be making through manipulation of perception. Mostly, it is no one's intention to fool us but what we see is different from the underlying reality.

If the US acts out of an idealistic impulse to bring peace to the world, this is often perceived as 'self-interest'. There are all sorts of conspiracy theories about how the world is really run by a small group of bankers and corporations.

For politicians it is very important to 'manage' perceptions. Should there be a problem or a scandal, it is necessary to play down the issue. If there is a constructive initiative, it is important that everyone sees it is a constructive initiative – and also who has taken the initiative.

The world we perceive is the world we live in.

Most people believe that their perception is being manipulated by advertising. And yet, to see the true value in an offered product or service, you need the creativity of advertising.

The quality of a great painting is that it allows the viewers to see life in a stronger way. The artist has captured the significant moment or expression.

In the UK, when a businessman is given a knighthood or other honour, the general perception is that he has donated funds to the party in power. It is only rarely that the award is seen to be based on individual merit. This perception is soundly based.

Whose Interest?

Something happens or some action is taken. In whose interest is this being done?

A corporation undertakes what appears to be a public-spirited gesture. Is this for the purpose of publicity?

A rock star is photographed visiting a home for the disabled. Is this really an attempt to help the disabled or a publicity stunt?

Sometimes it is difficult to tell what the truth really is. In practice, it is usually a mixture of self-interest and philanthropy. What matters is how things are perceived.

A paranoid person will logically interpret everything along the lines of the paranoia. The car is parked just there for a reason. That telephone call fits into the scheme. Why was that person in the corner of the restaurant looking at me? It all seems very logical.

Those who protest against globalisation do not do so because people in poorer countries are being given jobs they would not have had. The protest is not against these people being paid. The protest is on the basis that 'big business' is doing these things for its own sake. Big business is doing this to make even more money. The workers in the developing country are being exploited and are not being paid a proper wage.

The protest is not against what is happening but against the 'perceived' reason as to why it is happening (more profits for business).

It is quite true that outsourcing to a developing country means a loss of jobs in developed countries. This might be a valid basis for protest but such a protest would mean denying jobs to people in poorer countries, and that seems selfish.

Negative Perceptions

As with previous value medals, there are a lot of negative brass medal values. Something has happened and is being perceived in a negative way. It is important to be aware of that.

Some new product or project is planned. What might be the negative perceptions?

The US Secretary of State goes on television to urge young people to use condoms. Such use reduces the risk of unwanted pregnancies and HIV. The intention is very worthwhile. But some people perceive it in a negative sense. By advocating the use of condoms, that person is advocating – or at least condoning – sexual activity. That person should have been promoting abstinence from sexual activity.

It is important to foresee possible negative perceptions. It is important to see existing negative perceptions – and to seek to put them right.

For reasons such as these the exploration of perceptual values is very important. That is the role of the brass value medal.

Shaping Perceptions

There need be nothing dishonest about shaping perceptions. If you want people to see things in a certain way, you may need to shape perceptions. Advertising people do it all the time.

What has your seaside resort got to offer holiday-makers? How can you get people to perceive it this way?

What has your dating service got that is of real value? How can you get people to perceive this value?

What is different about your political candidate? How can you get the electors to see, and appreciate, this difference?

Dishonesty is easy to point out and to publicise. But how do you publicise 'honesty'? You can point out that the other candidates are dishonest (if they are). It is difficult, however, to put across the perception of honesty. You can portray the candidate as a 'man of the people', with the implication that this includes honesty. You might even seek to establish the slogan of 'Honest Jim' without much to support it.

Credibility

If you cannot trust your own perceptions, if you suspect that you are being fooled, then you might want to trust someone else's perception.

How do you know that this toothpaste is as good as it claims to be? If a famous film star endorses the product then you believe in that endorsement. The endorsing person is an admirable character and a role model, so what that person says must be true. The fact that this person might be paid a large amount of money for the endorsement does not seem to matter.

Selective Perception

We cannot be aware of everything around us all the time, so perception is almost always selective. We pick out what suits our purpose and our interest.

If you believe someone in the office to be a trouble-maker, you will perceive all those remarks which support this prejudice. If you believe that one ethnic group is different from another, you will perceive all those points which support that difference. You will ignore the points that show no difference.

A jealous person will perceive all their partners' activities that support the suspicion.

In a restaurant you choose the dishes that suit you from the menu. In real life our perception selects those things that suit our preconceptions, our needs and our emotions.

It is not that we see things clearly and objectively and then choose what we want. It is different from the restaurant analogy in this respect. In the restaurant we see the alternatives objectively and clearly and then choose what we want. With selective perception we see only what suits us. We simply do not see other things.

Different Points of View

The brass medal 'value scan' needs to take into account different points of view. The perceptions of these different parties may vary widely.

Those advocating sexual abstinence would object to the promotion of condoms.

Those having to deal with unwanted pregnancies and the spread of HIV would welcome the promotion of condoms.

Certain religious groups would also condemn the use of condoms.

What is positive for one group can be negative for another group. The brass medal 'value scan' needs to explore the different points of view to get the different perceptions.

What Are Your Brass Medal Values?

As in earlier chapters, you may want to list other brass medal values you find relevant.

ADDITIONAL BRASS MEDAL VALUES:

_____

_____

_____

_____

_____

_____

_____

_____

_____

_____

_____

_____

_____

_____

_____

_____

_____

_____

_____

Summary

1 People react to the real world of their perceptions, not to the true world.

2 In planning any project or activity it is important to scan for brass medal values. How will this be perceived?

3 Sometimes it may be a matter of countering an undeserved negative perception. Sometimes it may be a matter of putting right a deserved negative perception. Sometimes it may be a matter of shaping perceptions so that people come to see true value.

4 Selective perception means that we may see only what fits our emotions, preconceptions and prejudices.

5 In scanning for brass medal values it is important to consider different parties and different points of view. What might be the different perceptions?

11 ●●●●●●

VALUE SENSITIVITY

Our minds have been programmed from an early age to think critically. We are not taught 'value sensitivity' – to see the values in an idea. As we will see in this chapter, becoming more value-sensitive opens the door to creative thinking.

Criticism

The purpose of education is to teach young people how things are and how they were (history). Young people need to learn what is right and what is true. Any deviation from the 'proper' answer is marked down and regarded as wrong.

Criticism forms a large part of the teacher's behaviour. That is hardly surprising given the teacher's appointed role in education.

Parents are also involved in criticism, pointing out mistakes, punishing wrong behaviour and indicating dangers.

Both in school and later in college or university, a

lot of emphasis is put on 'critical thinking'. The word 'critical' comes from the Greek word for judge, *kritikos*. Judgment thinking accepts what is right and points out what is wrong.

The traditional and esteemed habit of argument and debate is much concerned with proving the other party wrong and proving their 'case' to be weak.

In real life there are rules and laws to be obeyed. There are penalties for getting things wrong.

Guilt is a strong factor both in families and in communities. Some groups put a stronger emphasis on guilt than do others. Guilt is a way of getting people to behave as they should.

Then there are real dangers to be avoided. If you cross the road without care you risk being killed by a car. If you do not handle electrical appliances with care you risk being electrocuted.

If you make mistakes at work you may get into trouble. You would certainly damage your chances of promotion.

Danger Sensitivity

For all the above reasons, it is not surprising that we develop a high sensitivity to danger. This means a sensitivity to mistakes, doing things the wrong way, risk, problems, and so on.

Our minds are finely tuned to seeing the faults and dangers in what is before us.

Imagine a boardroom full of very experienced and highly paid people. Someone is making a presentation. What is everyone else thinking? They are sitting there waiting to find some point to criticise in what is being said. If they can find such a point then they can contribute to the following discussion. This is the only game they know (because they have not been trained in parallel thinking).

A new idea is suggested at a meeting. Immediately everyone concentrates on the faults and weaknesses in the idea. They point out why it is not practical. They point out that the benefits are slight. They point out that the cost of implementation is large. They do what years of education and training have taught them to do. They show a high degree of 'danger sensitivity'.

Similarly, new ideas in your personal life can meet with criticism from yourself and others. You want to move to a bigger house – what about the increased mortgage repayments? You want to take up writing as a hobby – you probably don't have enough talent . . .

There is the underlying belief that all you have to do is avoid danger and making mistakes. If you do that then momentum and the natural course of events will take you forward. This belief fails to recognise the *values* of ideas.

Unseen Value

It is bad enough when everyone is only too ready to criticise a new idea as soon as it is presented. But there is something even worse.

I have sat in on many creative meetings which were called specifically to generate new ideas. New ideas have indeed been generated. But no one has been able to see the value in the new idea. This does not apply only to the other people – even the person who thought of the idea is unable to see its full value! This has happened many times.

Why does this happen? The reason is that we are trained and tuned to see danger but we are not trained or tuned to see value.

I would go so far as to say that creative effort is a waste of time if those taking part have not developed the habit of 'value sensitivity'.

> **Values are not always obvious. Values do not always stare us in the face. Sometimes values have to be detected. Sometimes there is a sudden insight which sees the values in an idea.**

New ideas are often full of unseen values.

We are not as sensitive to values as we are to danger. We do not have an automatic 'value scan'.

Elimination

A young woman has the luxury of too many suitors. How does she decide between them? Which one is she going to marry?

She could lay out the strong points of each suitor. One is handsome. One is rich. One is great fun. One is super sexy (these qualities may overlap). In practice it seems that this method does not work too well.

There is another method. This time the young woman focuses on the faults or deficiencies of each suitor. This one is selfish. This one has bad breath. This one is a bully. This one is lazy. By progressively eliminating the unsuitable suitor the young woman makes up her mind – provided she does not go too far and eliminate them all.

A motorist with a choice of roads to take seeks to eliminate the 'wrong' roads so that he or she can take the right road.

Faced with many alternatives we seek to eliminate the alternatives by focusing on their dangers. This makes action much simpler.

This is yet another practical reason why our minds and our thinking tend to be 'negatively oriented'.

Because of these natural and practical tendencies, we need to make a deliberate effort to develop value sensitivity.

The Value Scan

The Six Value Medals provide a convenient framework for a value scan. We make a quick search under each medal to see what values we find.

Some people will claim that they do this anyway. That may be so. In my experience, however, those who claim to do such things instinctively and subconsciously are in fact fooling themselves.

On one occasion I asked a roomful of top women executives if it might be a good idea to pay women 15 per cent more than men for doing the same job. Eighty-five per cent of those present were in favour of the idea. I then asked them to apply a formal future scan: immediate consequences, short-term, middle-term and long-term consequences. After doing this, the number in favour dropped to just 15 per cent. All those senior executives would have claimed that they always looked fully at consequences.

> **Doing something formally and deliberately may be very different from believing that you do it.**

'Look at all the values,' is a general request.

'What are the gold medal values here?' is a much more specific request.

The value medals provide a formal framework for a full value scan or a request for a specific type of value.

Habit

Once the Six Value Medals framework has been internalised then it can become a habit to look for values in any situation. There may not be a need to do a full value scan on each occasion. There can be a priority of values.

12

CONFLICTS AND PRIORITIES

Prioritising Values

Which is more important, your health or your pleasure?

Which is more important, your looks now or your looks in 20 years' time?

Which is more important, your reputation or your success?

In each case it may seem easy to decide, but it is not. People smoke cigarettes knowing it is bad for their health. Women lie in the sun and get tanned knowing that in 20 years' time their skin will not look good. Executives make decisions that may lead to immediate success but damage their reputation in the process.

There are always priorities of values but they are not consistent. You may claim that you would always put gold medal values first, but if this is going to inter-fere with profitability (silver medal, Chapter 6), you may change your mind.

Priorities depend on circumstances to some extent. To a much larger extent they depend on the degree or size of the values involved. Something may be worth doing if there is a big increase in brass medal values (perception, Chapter 10) but a small impact on silver medal values (Chapter 6). On the contrary, a small increase in profits is not worthwhile if there is a big negative environmental impact (wood medal, Chapter 9).

The value-scanning approach is usually much more flexible and pragmatic than moral values alone. With moral values, you are supposed to adhere to them no matter what the circumstances might be and no matter what there is to gain by abandoning the values.

There are those who argue that gold medal values and wood medal values are close to moral values and should therefore take priority. Some people do attempt to run their organisations in this way.

With priorities, some values take precedence over others or acquire more importance. The priority values may decide or at least influence the course of action.

For example, say you want a new career because your current occupation makes you unhappy. In looking to make a change your values are gold medal ones (Chapter 5). However, the job you want to do pays a lower salary (Silver medal, Chapter 6), which will affect your income and your family's budget (wood medal, Chapter 9). You need to work out how you prioritise these values before you act.

Conflict of Values

With conflict, there is an actual clash of values. If you choose one value, you create negative values some- where else.

If there is a fixed budget and you spend more on promotion, you have less to spend on fixing the car park.

If you are investing in new products you may have less to spend on increasing wages.

The conflict between personal values and the values of society is always ongoing.

The conflict between moral values and more world- ly values is ever present.

It is the purpose of culture and education to make it easier to deal with such conflicts of value. You just have to do 'the right thing'.

If your personal values have shifted to 'what you can get away with' then matters are much more complex.

It is always difficult to quantify moral or ethical considerations. The simple rule of thumb is not to do anything which goes against your personal moral and ethical values.

There are, however, conflicts where none of the values are moral or ethical in the strict sense of the words. These are more difficult situations because there is no simplifying rule.

The best you can do is lay out as clearly as possible

the conflicting values and then see if there is a superior value which might affect your choice.

If there is no superior value (such as bottom-line considerations or silver medal values, Chapter 6) then you choose between the values depending on your view of how things might turn out.

If you are working with others, you first seek agreement on the values that have been identified. Then you can look for suggestions as to the way forward.

Where there is a conflict of values the best approach is not to make a simple choice but to try to 'design' a way forward.

For example, say you have inherited some money. It is enough for you to spend on a holiday of a lifetime or to pay off your debts. Here the conflict is between gold (Chapter 5) and silver (Chapter 6) medal values: something you would really enjoy and remember for the rest of your life versus financial security. You could decide which value is more important to you or you could design a way forward, such as paying off some of your debts and having a less expensive holiday.

13

DESIGN

Design is as important as analysis. Yet we spend a great deal of educational thinking on analysis and virtually nothing on design.

Design means putting known things together to create new value.

Problem-Solving

Traditionally we seek to solve problems by identifying the cause and then seeking to remove the cause. This method works well in about 65 per cent of cases. There are times, however, when we cannot find the cause. There are times when there are so many causes that we cannot remove them all. There are times when we do find the cause but cannot remove it because it may be human nature itself.

A big hall had been built to house an international film festival. A few days before the opening of the festival there was a typhoon and the hall was flooded to a depth of a few feet. The organisers called in the engineers. What could be done? The engineers reckoned there would not be time to drain and dry the hall. So what did they do? They brought together a large number of carpenters who made box-like structures. The water was left there and the festival took place with people sitting on a platform over the water.

> If the cause cannot be removed it may be necessary to 'design' a way forward, leaving the cause in place.

This may seem cosmetic or 'papering over the cracks' but it need not be so. It can be a genuine solution. Most of the major problems in the world will not be solved by yet more analysis (which is all they ever get). There is a need to design a way forward.

Conflict Resolution

We seek to solve conflicts through legal means. One party is seen to have justice on its side so that party wins. There can be arbitration where an independent person decides on the way forward. There can be the usual battle of argument and negotiation from which a compromise may emerge.

What is needed is a greater emphasis on design. The needs and fears of both sides are taken into account and then an attempt is made to design a way forward.

There is a method of conflict resolution in which the two parties never meet. Each party informs the other party of its fears, needs and views of the future. Each party then 'designs' a way forward that would be fair to both parties. A judge or a panel then chooses what appears to be 'the fairest' design. If both parties design towards the 'reasonable', it probably does not much matter which design is chosen. If one party turns in an extreme design it is unlikely that design will be chosen.

It is possible that design is not much favoured because our methods of law and of government put all the emphasis on analysis and argument.

Conflicting Values

There are two important points about design:

1 *It is always worth seeking to design a way forward.*
2 *It is not always possible to reach a satisfactory design.*

Whenever there is a conflict of values, you can try to choose between the conflicting values. Or you can seek to design a way forward.

If an increase in the price of a product is deemed necessary (silver medal value, Chapter 6) but it is felt that this will have a negative perceptual value (brass medal value, Chapter 10) you might seek to add to the volume of the product or change the product in some small way so that it is no longer the same product at a higher price.

Decisions which appear as yes/no or either/or decisions at first sight often need not be so. Some effort at design may change the whole picture.

For some reason an improvement in the quality of a product means that a smaller variety of choice may be offered. So there is a conflict between quality of the product and quality of the customer's choice. One way forward is to continue to offer both types: the current product in a wider range; the better quality product at a higher price in a restricted range.

With a cruise line the lowering of price to attract a larger market may suggest a reduction in standards. The inclusion of a superior restaurant where meals could be purchased at much reduced prices (compared to the equivalent restaurant on shore) might reconcile the conflicting values.

Design requires creative thinking and lateral thinking. There may need to be new concepts or, at least, the modification of traditional concepts. With design there is an exploration of alternatives and possibilities.

A design is successful if it allows the conflicting values to be enjoyed. It may be that the full value cannot be enjoyed but enough of it remains to make the design worthwhile.

Design is not just modification of 'what is' in a sort of compromise. Modification is usually weak and not enough. Design demands a design phase in which ideas are created and explored before they are applied to the value conflict.

14

VALUE SIZE

How large are the values?
How significant are the values?

Not all values are equal. Some values are larger or more important than others. Yet there is not really a suitable word to describe the 'extent' or 'size' of values.

Why should this matter?

It matters for very practical reasons. If there is a choice between two alternatives and one alternative offers much 'larger' values than the other, that may affect your choice.

If taking some action has value and not taking the action also has value, you may want to compare the importance or 'size' of the values involved.

If you shorten the working week to 35 hours, as has been done in France, that will make workers happier (gold medal values), but how much happier? There will be a cost (silver medal values), but that is easier to calculate. The cost may be much greater for small businesses than for larger ones.

Investing in a new product takes time, money and management resources. What are the benefits likely to be? How large will the benefits be? There might be increased sales. The market position of the company might improve to make it the brand leader. At the same time, the advantage may be temporary as the competition will come in with a 'me-too' product. How do you quantify the benefits? How do you quantify risk?

Figures

You can put a figure on the estimated promotional cost of a new product. You cannot put a figure on increased management stress and anxiety. You cannot put a figure on the likelihood of a competitor copying, and how soon that might happen.

Where you can put a figure on one type of value – usually cost – but cannot put a figure on another type of value, how can you make a decision? The cost of setting up a new office in a certain country can be calculated. The effect that office will have on sales is more open-ended.

You may be able to calculate the total market size for a type of product. You can then estimate the proportion of that market you might reasonably take. This is a guess. So is your estimate of what the competitors might do. If they lower their prices then your profits might be eliminated.

Direct past experience and the experience of others can help. Comparison with related activities may help.

In the end it is clear that some types of value can be quantified but others cannot.

Four Degrees of Value

Although it may not be possible to put a definite figure on some values, we can still have a subjective sense of the size of that value.

You might, for example, divide your friends into four subjective categories:

1   *Your very close friends whom you like a lot and want to see often.*
2   *Good friends.*
3   *Acquaintances whom you like but would not make a great deal of effort to see or entertain.*
4   *People you have met at one time or another and might say 'Good morning' to if you bumped into each other in the street.*

Such a subjective division would not be too hard to do. There could, however, be some difficult cases. For example, there might be someone you have met only briefly but really liked. Would that person go into category one or category four? Is 'liking' a basis for the categories or should the categories be based on the actual 'reality' of the relationship?

With any subjective categorisation there are likely to be borderline cases. If you make the basis of the categorisation very clear then some of the borderline cases disappear. In the end, you can always put a difficult case into both categories.

Suppose you had to divide the people you know into four sizes. You had to do this subjectively without using a tape measure or weighing scales.

There would be the 'big' people. These people would be unusually large in height, in weight or in both.

Then there would be the 'normal' people who were not too big and not too small.

Next would be the 'small' people. In practice, this would mean the 'short' people.

Finally, there would be the 'tiny' people. Such people would be exceptionally small or petite.

In a restaurant you could look at a menu and divide the dishes into four categories:

1 *exceptional and very attractive*
2 *good standard food*
3 *not very appealing*
4 *no interest at all*

The last category is not really negative but simply indicates a lack of interest.

We can now seek to apply the same four-point scale of categories to values.

As in the above examples, the application of the categories is always subjective. This means the scale is applied from your point of view. How do you see the value? If you wish to shift to another point of view then you should state this explicitly.

Now, from the consumers' point of view . . .
But, from the government's point of view . . .

Strong Values

> These are large values. These are strong values. These are important values.

Only big and significant values get put into this category. Just as there is no doubt that a person is 'large', so there should be no doubt that a value is a strong value. If there is the slightest doubt then the value does not get put into this category. So the category might be: 'strong without any doubt'.

The gold medal value of increasing wages significantly might qualify as 'strong'.
The silver medal value of cutting supplier prices by more than 20 per cent might qualify as 'strong'.
The steel medal value of completely smear-proof ink might qualify as strong.

The glass medal value of insurance that you could pick up in any newsagent would qualify as strong.

The wood medal value of a shift to wind farm electricity might qualify as strong.

The brass medal value of reducing the price of pharmaceuticals for poorer countries would qualify as strong.

Sound Values

Sound values are not as strong as strong values.

In practice, there are many more 'sound' values than 'strong' values, just as there are many more normal people than large people.

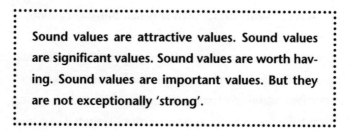

Sound values are attractive values. Sound values are significant values. Sound values are worth having. Sound values are important values. But they are not exceptionally 'strong'.

Repainting and redecorating the cafeteria might be a sound gold medal value.

Calling in a management consulting group might be a sound silver medal value.

Increasing the warranty period on electrical appliances might be a sound steel medal value.

Offering a free glass of wine with every dinner might be a sound glass medal value.

Using recycled paper for packaging might be a sound wood medal value.

Advising customers of possible health hazards might be a sound brass medal value.

Weak Values

Weak values are definite values but they are not very powerful. This does not mean they can be neglected. In many areas only weak values are available and you have to work with these. It is no use hoping for strong values or even sound values if these are hard to come by.

> **A weak value on its own is weak. But a collection of weak values adds up to something significant.**

It is only in comparison with more powerful values that the weak values appear weak. The 'village Venus' is attractive enough, and it is only in comparison with nightclub beauties that she may appear homely.

Calling people by their name might be a weak gold medal value (some might consider this 'strong').

Loading more cartons on to every truck might be a weak silver medal value.

Including on-board tips in the price of a cruise might be a weak steel medal value.

Making it easier to open a cereal packet might qualify as a weak glass medal value (in some cases this might even be strong).

Giving a donation to an environmental group might be a weak wood medal value.

Making the print on a package more readable might be a weak brass medal value.

Remote Values

There is a change here. 'Remote' is not on the same scale as the other degrees of value. Remote does not refer to the size or strength of the value.

> 'Remote' refers to the small possibility of something happening. That value itself might actually be strong – but there is only a remote possibility of it happening. The value is simply not very likely.

There is just a possibility that this may happen.
It could be a real value – it is just not very likely.

Asking workers to nominate the most creative person in the group might encourage creativity. That is a remote gold medal value.

Encouraging store customers to complain might just

turn up some new suggestions. That is a remote silver medal value.

Labelling fruit as 'big' or 'small' might offer a remote steel medal value.

Putting a loop in the cap of toothpaste tubes might be a remote glass medal value.

Sponsoring street refuse bins might be a remote wood medal value.

Admitting a minor error might provide a remote brass medal value.

Negative Values

Exactly the same scale can be applied to negative values.

That is a strong steel negative value. We certainly have to take that into account.
All those are sound silver negative values.
I agree, but that is only a weak gold negative value.
It is not very likely to happen. That is only a remote brass negative value.

It would not be necessary to keep repeating the nature of the value. Once it was clear that you were discussing gold medal values then you would just talk about 'values'. It would only be at a switch point that you would state which 'medal values' you were considering.

Assessment

Once the four degrees of value have been learned and internalised, there is a sort of instant assessment. How large is this value? Sometimes the assessment is easy but at other times there is a need to think more carefully about the value.

There is a story of a French farmer who asked his son to sort a pile of apples into big apples and small apples. The farmer went off to market. When he returned the son had sorted the apples into two piles. The father thanked his son and then put all the apples back together again. The son was furious at the waste of his day's work. The father explained:

'I really wanted you to throw out the bad apples – which you have done. But by asking you to make a much more difficult selection you had to pay more attention to each apple.'

In some ways the 'degrees' of value force us to think more clearly about each value we come across.

15

BENEFITS AND COSTS

Values are sometimes seen as 'benefits minus cost'. While this may be logically correct, it is psychologically weak.

Benefits refer to value in a relationship. A gold bar is of a certain value to a jeweller. A gold bar is of a different value to an investor who wants a hedge against inflation and may never see the bar. A gold bar is of a different value to someone who wants to use the heavy weight of the bar as a door stop.

Benefits refer only to this relationship value. What are the benefits to me or my organisation? 'Values' is a much broader term and refers to the relationship value, to the intrinsic value, to the potential value and even the undiscovered value.

> So looking for benefits is a very self-centred exercise. Looking for values is more objective. What is the value here? Rather than: what is the value for me? This means that we make much more effort to find the full value.

Benefits become important when we make decisions. So the traditional definition could be changed to 'benefits equal value minus cost'.

The cost of using the value might vary from organisation to organisation and from person to person. A travel company that is already organising travel might find it easy to organise educational holidays. An educational company might find it much more expensive to do the same. The market value in each case is the same but the benefits would be very different.

A biscuit-making company would find it easy to introduce 'bran biscuits'. The production machinery, distribution chain and branding are all in place. A grain company that produces bran would find it much more expensive and difficult. The value (to consumers) is the same but the benefits to the organisation differ.

You choose to do something if there are benefits in it for you. So benefits are more 'relative' than values.

Decisions

Many factors go into decision-making. These include strategy, policy, cost, resources, personalities, risk assessment, alternatives and culture.

There are many levels of risk:

Can this be done at all?
Can we do it?

Can we do it at an acceptable price?
Will it work in the marketplace?
What are the potential problems?
How might competitors respond?

Most decisions are made on the concept of 'fit':

Does this fit our 'risk' culture?
Does this fit our structure?
Does this fit our resources?
Does this fit our strategy?
Does this fit our ethics?
Does this fit our budget?

It is obvious that judging 'fit' is much more practical than seeking to judge value in itself.

The danger of 'fit' is that it is always based on the past. A tailor makes a suit to fit your size at the moment. There is no room for growth.

A young man decides he likes blondes. One day at a party he sees a beautiful redhead. What does he do? Does he reject the beauty, or does he change his selection frame?

When new opportunities emerge, can we see them with their full value or only in terms of fit with our preconceived ideas? The history of business is full of examples going either way. There is the inability to change frames as with Xerox, who did much of the pioneering work with computers. There is the ability to change frames as with Rank-Xerox in the UK, which went from a flour-milling operation to something quite different.

The research departments of many large organisations are full of very valuable ideas that are never used. Much money and work has gone into the development of these ideas. They are not used because other ideas seem to fit the priorities better. They are not used because they do not 'fit' the decision frame in use.

In decision-making five factors seem to emerge:

1. *Full examination of the values of each alternative.*
2. *Full examination of the negative values of each alternative.*
3. *The risk factor.*
4. *The 'fit' with the organisation or individual.*
5. *The personalities involved.*

Negative Values

Costs come under negative values. If the costs are high then there is a high (silver medal) negative value. Some costs may be spelled out and quantified. There are some costs that cannot easily be quantified. Management stress and time are not easy to assess. Even less easy to assess is the time diverted from other activities. The non-quantifiable costs can still be assessed as strong, sound, weak or remote (see Chapter 14).

There may be many negative values apart from traditional costs. The new product may cannibalise existing sales. The new product may risk the brand image. The new product may arouse a strong competitive response.

It is not really a matter of subtracting the negative values from the other values in order to assess benefits. Both sets of values need to be considered in parallel – on the same map.

There is a place for detailed cost considerations. If the estimated increase in revenue does not exceed the needed investment, the benefits are not there – no matter how high the perceived value.

The value triangle (Chapter 17) and the value map (Chapter 18) supply frameworks to enable you to consider all the values – positive and negative – in every decision you make.

16

SOURCES OF VALUE

Some sources of value are fairly obvious. Others are not quite so easy to see unless we are in the habit of looking for them. In this chapter I want to focus on these less obvious sources and types of value. There is considerable overlap between the types. This simply means that you might view the same thing from two perspectives.

Communication Values

Communication is such an obvious value that it hardly needs mentioning. The transfer of information from one point to another is the basis of many businesses.

Most organisations, however, are unaware of how poor their internal communications might be. If everyone does only what he or she is supposed to do, there might be little cross-communication. Communication that is driven only by need excludes communication that generates change opportunities.

Permission

This can be a very significant type of value. A plot of land with a building permit is much more valuable than the plot without the permit. In certain countries a permit or licence is required for business activities. A restaurant with an alcohol licence is more valuable than one without. The permission to land aeroplanes at a certain airport (landing slots) can be extremely valuable.

There are all sorts of licences that can be obtained and have value. There are licences for patents and for intellectual property of any sort.

Permission may be needed to make sense of other values which cannot develop without the permission. Permission, itself, may be the key value.

Permission implies that some other party may be involved. On a personal level, there are times when you may need to give permission to yourself to do something – or to think something.

Gateway

No one has to give you permission to learn French. Learning French may be the 'gateway' to doing business in France.

There are examination which are gateways to taking up different courses at university. In many subject areas the mathematics requirements are unnecessarily high in these days of computers. So people who are not good at mathematics take up law. Hence the huge popularity of the law faculty in the USA where there are 27 times as many lawyers per head of population as in Japan.

Gateways are entrance requirements. You have to go through the gateway to enter a particular universe. Hiring someone skilled in youth marketing may be the gateway to a new market segment.

You need to choose the gateway and want to get through it. You can use your own skills or, in some cases, hire the skills you need.

Gateways are a form of value. There is a difference between the first IT specialist you take on board and the second. The first one opens the gateway. The second one supports that activity.

Enabler Values

An enabler value simply enables you to do something. Enablers are wider in scope than permission or gateway values. Being able to outsource production of a key component to China may enable you to compete at a lower cost.

Acquiring a rapid way of testing electronic products may enable you to speed up production. In the pharmaceutical industry, having a way of testing the effects of drugs enables more rapid research to be undertaken in that field.

On a personal level, studying for professional exams may enable you to gain a promotion. Joining a gym may enable you to get fit and lose weight.

Enablers are not quite like the missing piece in a jigsaw. In some cases you can proceed without the enabler but it may take much longer. In other cases you may not be able to proceed at all without the enabler.

Catalyst Values

In chemistry, a catalyst holds other chemical elements in such a way that they can combine and proceed on their way as a new compound. The catalyst is unchanged and continues to carry out this 'joining function'.

Someone introduces you to a valuable business contact. That person has acted as a catalyst to put you together with the new contact. The catalyst no longer takes part in the process. Dating agencies provide a classic catalyst service.

The initiation of a new product may act as a catalyst, bringing together a group that goes on to work on better products, dropping the original product.

Enhancer Values

The value of any meeting is enhanced by training in the parallel thinking method of the Six Hats (see page

29). The meetings take less time. The outcome is more powerful. People agree on the outcome. Every person in the meeting has a chance to give his or her best thinking to the matter. Difficult people, difficult egos and personal agendas have less impact on meetings. If decisions which could have been reached in 30 days are now reached in two days, the 'productivity' of the meeting has been greatly enhanced.

A loudspeaker system enhances or amplifies the volume of the human voice. Word-of-mouth publicity enhances the value of advertising.

A hot summer enhances the process of selling beer. A cold winter does the same for overcoats.

Accelerator Values

An accelerator is really an enhancer that operates only in the time dimension. In certain countries it used to be the case that a bribe to the right official would accelerate the permissions process. That behaviour is now generally discouraged.

The opening up of the Suez Canal had an accelerator value on trade between Asia and Europe.

Restructuring departments can have an accelerator value on product development. The creation of new posts and task forces may also have an accelerator function.

I once suggested to the public service in Singapore that they should introduce a 'speed-up unit'. If things were taking too long, someone could ask that unit to look into the delay and put pressure on the relevant department to speed things up. This is not to suggest that the Singapore authorities are slow: quite the contrary. Many other authorities could benefit even more from the same idea.

Problem-Solving

A problem is a pain, an obstacle, a block and always a negative value. Problem-solving is not usually seen as value enhancement but more as part of maintenance. Problem-solving needs to be seen more clearly as a value delivery mechanism.

If solving a particular problem does not deliver much value then there may not be much point in solving that problem!

The problem of theft by the staff in restaurants is a serious negative value with a considerable cost. Solving this problem can make the difference between a profitable restaurant and an unprofitable one.

Passengers who have checked in their baggage but then arrive late at the departure gate hold up flights, wreck connections and disrupt schedules. If this problem could be solved, both the silver and steel medal values would be greatly increased (for the airline and also for the passengers).

Removing Bottlenecks

This is another obvious value. We tend to think of bottlenecks in supply or in the production process. Yet far more serious bottlenecks may occur, out of sight, in the decision-making process.

Bottlenecks may be caused by too much seeking to flow through a restricted channel. This is a volume-type bottleneck. It can usually be solved by restructuring. The other type of bottleneck is caused by a very inefficient flow channel with delays built into it.

It used to be said that the Food and Drug Administration (FDA) in the US was deliberately slow in approving new drugs so that they would be tried elsewhere in the world and their harmful effects noted in other countries first. In this way the decision of the FDA could be based on large-scale 'trials' of the drug in question.

It is alleged that American banks take an extraordinarily long time to clear foreign cheques because they enjoy the interest of the money float in the meantime.

Bottlenecks are a negative value. Removing them through restructuring or reorganising is a positive value.

Mistakes

Everyone is always very keen to point out that mistakes are useful because we can learn from them. We can learn not to go down that road again. We can learn that we need a better infrastructure to introduce new products. We can learn that the bureaucratic process is too slow to deal with crises. We can learn that the wrong person is in a certain position.

There are basically two types of mistake:

1   *Something has been done in the wrong way which should have been done in the right way. A nurse giving too much of a medicine might be an example. Loading an airliner in Canada with as many litres as would have been done with gallons is an example (it actually happened at the switch-over from gallons to litres). Misreading the market mood might also be a mistake – but a more understandable one. Launching a new type of car too late may be another mistake which could have been avoided.*

2   *You do everything right but for some reason the project fails. It fails for reasons that would have been impossible to predict. There may have been a change in government regulations. There may have been a very sharp rise in supplier prices. A natural disaster or terrorist attack might have disturbed the market. These should not really be called mistakes. They are: 'reasonable ventures that failed for reasons that could not have been foreseen'. We badly need a new word for that. Otherwise people are very reluctant to try new things because they get blamed if the project 'fails'.*

With both types of 'mistake' we can seek to learn lessons. It might be a matter of having a backup system (not putting all your eggs in one basket) or a contingency plan. It might be a matter of 'hedging' so that whichever way the circumstances go, your project would benefit.

Competitors

Although 'ego' usually prevents us from seeing too much value in what our competitors are doing, there are values to be seen. Most of these values will have been seen by the competitor but some may not.

Sony's Betamax system was first in the market for video playing. But VHS took over the market, although technically it was no better (some say worse) than Betamax. It seems that the VHS group encouraged many other producers to use their system.

Competitors may do the hard part and prepare the market for something new. Then you come in with a me-too product.

It is said that the internet bookstore, Amazon, has not been keen to show profits too soon because a lot of competitors would have piled into the market. By investing in warehouses rather than showing profits, Amazon has built up a delivery system that would be hard to beat.

Failures

At a business meeting in Sweden I was once asked where ideas for new businesses might come from. I suggested a look at the bankruptcy files.

In these files would be ideas which would have been ahead of their times. With today's technology, such ideas might be valuable.

There may be other ideas which were indeed good ideas but the business was under-capitalised or poorly managed.

Bankruptcy does not always mean that the idea was poor.

Concepts

Concepts are very, very valuable. We totally underestimate the value of concepts.

In the future, value is not going to come from more and more technology. Value is going to come from 'value concepts' which use existing technology to deliver new value. At the moment our 'value concepts' are way behind our technological development.

That is why I am setting up a Value Design Laboratory to generate just such new concepts. Such concepts will not come from technical research but from lateral thinking and design thinking.

17

THE VALUE TRIANGLE

It is sometimes useful to see things instantly and at a glance. Reading ordinary language may be too slow a method of communication.

What is presented here is a very simple visual notation for a value scan. It shows at a glance how the six value medals score for a particular idea or project.

Using this notation you can get an instant impression of the 'value shape' of the idea. This allows you to sift rapidly through ideas and to focus only on those which seem promising.

The human mind is very good at perceiving patterns as a whole. Unlike with language, patterns do not have to be built up bit by bit, so the value shape can be perceived as a whole.

The Triangle

The triangle is made up of six equal circles. It is like a pyramid but, being two-dimensional, it is a triangle.

Each of the six circles represents one of the six

value medals. The positioning of the medals in the triangle is indicated below.

Silver Medal

This medal is at the top of the triangle. This does not mean it is necessarily the most important value. But every value scan is made from a certain point of view.

The point of view is usually that of the organisation or individual that is going to assess the values and then take action on that assessment. So the owner or initiator of the scan is the most interested in the scan.

Silver medal values refer to organisational values and are therefore the type of value most relevant to the user of the value triangle.

Although, throughout this book, silver medal values have been referred to as organisational values, they apply just as well when an 'individual' is the organisation. You can do a value scan for yourself. The silver medal values are now the ones which relate to your defined purpose in doing the scan. Remember that silver medal values are related to the purpose of the organisation.

Steel Medal

The steel medal is represented by the circle at the top left. This is because the 'quality' values are the delivered values and are very important.

Any action is designed to deliver quality as well as to benefit the party delivering the value. Customer values come under the steel medal.

If you are doing the value scan on a personal basis then the steel medal values are the values you get to enjoy. Since you are both operator and customer, there may be an overlap with silver medal values. You may buy toilet paper in bulk because it reduces the hassle of shopping frequently. At the same time you might get a better price.

If you give a party, you might enjoy giving the party but you might also make useful new friends (brought by your existing friends).

Gold Medal

The gold medal is represented by the top right circle of the triangle. It is indeed a superior and important value.

Gold medal values are human values. The gold medal, however, is not often the 'objective value'. It is not often that something is done specifically to generate gold medal values. Nevertheless, the gold medal values are important and do have to be taken into account, especially if they are negative.

A business functions to generate profits (and ensure its survival). Care and consideration for the employees is a high value but that is not usually the prime purpose of the business.

If you are doing a personal value scan then the gold medal values apply to the people around you: partners, colleagues, family, friends. How are their values affected by what you do?

Glass Medal

The glass medal is represented by the right circle on the bottom layer of the triangle.

Although creativity and innovation are very important, they are not a major factor in most activities. Vitamins are important but we do not live on vitamins. We eat the food that sustains us and pay serious attention to vitamins at the same time. So creativity and innovation need to be there but are not dominant in most matters.

Glass medal values hold the same position in a personal value scan as in a business value scan. It may be that in a particular instance the emphasis is mainly on creativity and new thinking, but in general this is not the case.

Wood Medal

The wood medal is in the centre of the bottom row. This symbolises the central position of environmental considerations. Our choices and actions affect our surroundings. The centre position on the bottom row has many surroundings.

At the same time, the wood medal values are not as dominant as the silver or steel medal values. Like the gold medal values, the wood medal values have to be taken into account. It is important not to cause negative wood medal values, just as it is important not to bring about negative gold medal values. In general, these are not 'driving values' but 'consideration values'.

For a personal value scan, the wood medal may refer to the environment in the usual broad sense, but it can also refer to your local environment. The people in that local environment will be considered under the gold medal, but everything else comes under the wood medal.

Brass Medal

The brass medal is represented by the left medal in the bottom row of the triangle.

This is the first circle you would come to if you were scanning across the page: it is the first part of the triangle. This is symbolic because perception is what you come across first.

When you are carrying out a personal scan, the brass medal is very significant. How will your actions and behaviour be seen? How will your actions and behaviour be seen by those close to you? What about the perceptions of the community? What about your reputation? For an individual, this is an important value medal.

Value Strength

In the value triangle the 'strength' or degree of values is shown by a number from 1 to 4, with 4 being the highest rating.

'Strong value' is given the number 4.
'Sound value' is given the number 3.
'Weak value' is given the number 2.
'Remote value' is given the number 1.

The appropriate estimated figure is inserted into the relevant circle. In this way you can tell at a glance the different value strengths for each value medal.

Negative Values

Exactly the same scoring system holds for negative values. This time, however, a 'minus sign' is placed before the figure.

So '−4' indicates a strong negative value. A remote negative value would be '−1'. Again, the number is placed in the appropriate circle corresponding to the relevant medal.

For the purpose of instant visibility, the minus sign can be converted into a large 'dot' placed before the negative value.

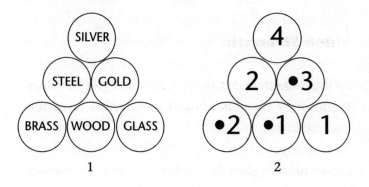

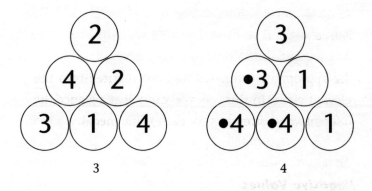

The illustration above shows four value triangles.

Figure 1 shows the positioning of each medal as discussed earlier. This positioning is always constant and can be committed to memory.

Figure 2 shows a value scan for a particular project. At once it can be seen that the project would greatly benefit the corporation (silver). The quality and customer values (steel) are present but weak. There is considerable negative impact on human values (gold). The environmental impact is slightly negative (wood). The way the project will be perceived is weakly negative (brass). The innovation element is slight (glass). Should the project go ahead? Probably not.

Figure 3 shows another value scan for a new product idea. The innovation value is high (glass) and so is the customer value (steel). Perception is good (brass). Gold medal values are positive and so is the environmental impact (wood). The benefit to the corporation is weak (silver). Should the project go ahead? This would depend on the balance between the investment needed and the value of market impact.

Figure 4 shows a disastrous value scan. The perceptual impact is strongly negative (brass). The environmental impact is strongly negative (wood). The delivered quality is negative (steel). The innovation component is remote (glass) as is the gold medal value. The value to the organisation is sound but not strong (silver). In view of the strong negatives, the project would probably not go ahead.

Comparison

The value scan gives only a summary or first impression. You would then need to look in more detail at the actual nature of the values involved.

When several individuals are each asked to do their own value scan, the value triangles produced can be compared and discussed. The reasons behind different estimates of value can then be brought out into the open. This provides a clearer and more powerful basis for value discussions.

18

THE VALUE MAP

This is another way of presenting a value scan. It is much more detailed than the 'value triangle' as seen in the previous chapter. While the purpose of the value triangle is to give a summary or first impression of the values involved, the value map allows the different values to be detailed.

The value map is shown overleaf. Each side of the hexagon represents one of the value medals. The positioning of the medals is roughly similar to that in the value triangle.

Radiating outwards from the centre of the hexagon are four levels. These represent the degrees of value. The strongest values are placed nearest the centre of the hexagon and the remote values in the outermost layer. This symbolises 'closely' or 'remotely' related.

Listing

The numbers inserted on the map refer to the numbers on a list since it would be impossible to write

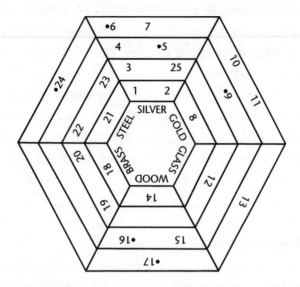

down the full value on the map. So number '8' refers to item '8' on a separate list.

You can scan the values in a number of ways.

You might focus on one medal first and go through the layers of value with regard only to that medal. For example, you may focus on glass medal values. What are the strong glass medal values? What are the sound, weak or remote glass values? Are there any negative glass medal values? The answers are then written down in a list. Then you move clockwise around the web doing the same for each medal in turn.

Alternatively, you can look at only the 'strong' values first and then move on to the strong values of the next medal, and so on around the hexagon. Next you move to the 'sound values' and go around again. You do this with all value layers.

Any new value that you think of, even if out of turn, can be added with the next number anywhere on the map (see number 25 for the silver medal in the diagram on page 154).

The actual list can be continuous, without regard to the different medals, as shown in the diagram. It is also possible to have a separate list for each medal so that all the values relating to that medal may be read at once.

Negative Values

As for the value triangle (Chapter 17), negative values can be shown by putting a large 'dot' in front of the figure – even though this refers just to a list number. This has been done in the diagram.

This allows a quick scan of the map. You note where the major values lie and you also note which of them are negative.

Sample List

The first part of a list is given here. It refers to the numbers given in the diagram.

The idea being 'value scanned' is the suggestion that a fast-food chain serve only 'starters'. Customers could order as many or as few as they liked, depending on their appetite.

1. *Fits very well with dieting and health food consciousness. (4)*
2. *Potentially a powerful brand in a well-established market segment. (4)*
3. *'Starters' are often cold so there is less cooking and less wastage. (3)*
4. *Much more variety than with traditional fast food. (2)*
5. *More skilled staff may be required to deal with different foods. (–2)*
6. *Difficult to assess the balance between the different items sold. Danger of over- or under-stocking. (–1)*
7. *Attractive if you want more variety than with the usual fast food. (1)*
8. *Much more motivating for the staff to deal with a variety of dishes. (4)*
9. *Confusion burden on staff and possibility of more complaints. (–2)*
10. *More prestigious for staff. (1)*
11. *Healthier eating for the staff themselves. (1)*
12. *etc.*

Note that in this list the 'degree' or strength of the value has been given in brackets after the value. The same strength rating is used as for the value triangle: strong is 4; sound is 3; weak is 2; remote is 1.

Joint Maps

A value map may be done by individuals and their efforts then compared, as with the value triangle (see page 143). There may be more value in a joint effort with everyone contributing and discussing each value as it is suggested.

A value map can be re-edited, tidied up and changed over time. There need be nothing fixed about it. Geographical maps are continually being updated as more information becomes available or the region changes.

If more information is needed at a particular point then a small question mark can be placed against that number on the map.

State of Thinking

The value map shows the current state of thinking about values in a particular area. Where are we at? The map is subjective but then much of the assessment of values is subjective because it refers to the future, about which we cannot be certain.

The map allows values to be put out in the open so that they can be looked at again and again and by anybody. The map is a way of externalising thinking.

●●●●●●

VICTERI TEAMS

Values are so important that they should not be left to everyone's background thinking. Values need direct and focused attention. That is the purpose of the VICTERI team.

V = Values
I = Ideas
C = Concepts

T = Target

E = Examine
R = Review
I = Innovate

An organisation may have one VICTERI team or a team for each division or product line. The team is made up of four to six people who will all be doing other jobs as well. The team meets to focus and think about values. They think as a team and also as individuals.

The team would use the value medal framework and other thinking methods, such as lateral thinking and the Six Hats. The team would report periodically.

The purpose of the team is to target values and to examine and review existing values. In addition there will be an effort to innovate either by modifying existing values or creating new ones.

For further information and instructions on how to run a VICTERI team please see:
www.edwarddebono.com/victeri

(Note: It is not coincidence that when pronounced VICTERI sounds like 'victory'.)

CONCLUSION

Everyone knows that values are important. Some people realise that values are going to become even more important than they have been before.

In a strongly competitive world, competence is becoming a commodity. Competence is essential but it is only a baseline. When everyone is equally competent, what then?

Information is another commodity. Information can be gathered or purchased. It is what you do with information that matters.

State-of-the-art technology is becoming another commodity (with a few exceptions). It is what you do with technology – the value concepts – that are going to matter as much as the technology itself.

The design of projects, products and services is a matter of creative thinking that focuses on value.

The decision whether to go ahead with a new project or product depends on value assessment.

The choice between different alternatives and opportunities in our personal lives depends on value assessment.

In all areas of thinking and action, value assessment is crucial.

Seeing Values

Although values are real, they are also vague and intangible, and it is difficult to think about them. This is largely a perceptual problem. How do we 'see' values?

This book puts forward a concrete 'framework' for looking at values and assessing them. The practicality of such frameworks has been shown by the very widespread use of the Six Thinking Hats framework in business, in law courts and in family discussions.

Perception and Communication

We need to be able to see things clearly and to communicate our perception to others. The Six Value Medals framework does exactly this.

Each of the 'medals' allows us to direct our attention to a different set of values. We can now do one thing at a time instead of trying to do everything at once. Tossing up one ball at a time is easier than seeking to juggle with six.

Different perceptions and assessments of value can now be compared and discussed. Attention is under our control instead of being pulled only to what appears 'interesting'.

Each medal suggests an 'appreciation' of the values present in a defined area: from gold medal human values to silver medal organisational values; from steel medal quality values to glass medal innovation values; from wood medal environmental concerns to brass medal 'appearance' values. The value spectrum is covered with the medals.

Visual Display

It is sometimes useful to be able to see things at a single glance rather than remembering a lot of language. Two very simple visual notations have been put forward in this book.

The 'value triangle' puts the different values forward in a simple notation which can be taken in at a glance.

The 'value map' is more detailed. The map allows both an instant assessment but also the possibility of following values up in more detail.

Both notations can be used on a personal level or for comparison between different people. The visual notations produced by individuals can be compared and discussed.

It is not enough to know that values are important. We need better ways of perceiving values, talking about them and assessing them. That is the best basis for action of any sort. This book provides you with the tools to do this.